How To Get
Commercial
Lawn Care
And
Snow Plow
Customers.

**From The Gopher Lawn Care Business Forum &
The GopherHaul Lawn Care Business Show**

By Steve Low

Table of Contents

INTRODUCTION

Welcome.

Hello and welcome to my book on how to get commercial lawn care and snow plow customers.

I put this book together because I know it can be so very difficult for newer lawn care, landscaping, or snow plow business owners to find out how to gain commercial customers. Do you just go in and knock on doors? Do you send them letters? How should they be approached?

All too often when people try things, they experiment once and if it doesn't give them the results they are looking for, they give up and think they just lacked some magical quality others who are successful must have that they don't.

Well there are no magical qualities, there are just certain tips and tricks we have seen that work over the years being discussed on the Gopher Lawn Care Business Forum and these are the tips I want to share with you.

Gaining new customers shouldn't be this hidden secret skill. It should be made readily available to you so that you can grow your business as big as you want, based on your desire and not based on luck or chance.

As you read through this book, you will see variations of certain methods pop up again and again. When you see that, it's because those methods being discussed work. The variations you see are little tweaks that business owners utilize to stand out from others. You can use them too, or take the basic skills you learn here and create your own tweaks to make them uniquely yours.

When you are finished reading this book, I hope you feel like you have a successful family member in the lawn care business that has shared with you a lifetime of what he has learned.

It has taken many years to compile all these insights and business lessons and there is no doubt in my mind, your business will grow because of it.

I want to thank all my friends on the Gopher Lawn Care Business forum who have talked with me over the years on these many topics. It is because of those people that came in, asked questions and shared answers, that we all are able to benefit today.

If you would like to read more about how to improve your lawn care or landscaping business, check out my many books on the topic. Visit my Gopher Lawn Care Business Forum at http://www.gopherforum.com and watch my GopherHaul Lawn Care Business Videos and Podcasts across the internet and on my GopherHaul Lawn Care Business & Marketing Blog at http://www.lawnchat.com.

And remember.. If you haven't started your business yet, what are you waiting for. If you don't start your business this year, you'll be at least a year older when you do. So get started today.

Sincerely,

Steve Low

Special Thanks to Gopher Lawn Care Software.

This book would not have been possible without the help and guidance of all our friends and business owners we have met over the years on our Gopher Forum.

Also thank you to the staff at Gopher Software for making all of this happen.

Lawn Care Software

PROBLEM: Scheduling & billing repetitive jobs is tedious and time consuming.

SOLUTION: Gopher Billing & Scheduling Software allows you to Quickly and Easily schedule jobs and create invoices.

Gopher Landscape Billing and Scheduling Software simplifies the task of scheduling your lawn care jobs and billing your customers. Simply set up your jobs at the beginning of the season and let Gopher handle the rest. With Gopher, you can print out a list of scheduled jobs for each day and then automatically print invoices after those jobs have been completed.

Download your free trial of Gopher Billing & Scheduling
Software at **http://www.gophersoftware.com**

Continue your reading.

I have more great information on running a lawn care business in my other books, "**Stop Lowballing! A Lawn Care Business Owner's Guide To Success.**"

Some of the topics discussed in the book: - How to start up your lawn care business. - Finding your niche and finding profits. - Lawn Care Equipment. - Pricing & Estimating Lawn Care Jobs. - Dealing With Customers. - Dealing With Employees. - Lawn Care Marketing Secrets. - Lawn Care Business Tips. - Getting Commercial Accounts without commercial references. - Pitfalls of Commercial Accounts. And more.

The GopherHaul Lawn Care Marketing & Landscaping Business Show Episode Guide. Topics discuss include: How to raise start up capital. Seasonal marketing ideas. What to do when your largest client leaves? What's better to use, postcards or brochures? How to build your customer base with referrals? Gain one customer then lose one customer. How to stop it? How to pre-qualify customers when they call? How to bid jobs. What should you include in a commercial lawn care bid? What newspaper ads work best? How to buy a lawn care business. Tips on buying used lawn care equipment. And much more.

How to get customers for your landscaping and lawn care business all year long. Volume 1. Anyone can start a lawn care business, the tricky part is finding customers. Learn how in this book. New lawn care business owners were polled and 33% of them said the toughest part about running their business was finding customers. This book shows you how to get new lawn care customers. Don't start from scratch and try to re-create the wheel. Learn what works and what doesn't.

Volume #1 discusses: Getting started, choosing a business name, harnessing employees to sell, community marketing ideas, free rentals to offer, hosting events to get exposure, volunteer projects to build goodwill, how to get residential and commercial customers (including sample letters). Bikini lawn care, getting in your local paper, marketing on price, publicity stunts & media attention, organic lawn care marketing, reaching out to realtors, turning hobbies into marketing ideas, seasonal marketing ideas that work.

How to get customers for your landscaping and lawn care business all year long. Volume 2.

Volume #2 discusses: The most effective lawn care business marketing methods. How to track your ads, the best ways to utilize: billboards, brochures, business cards, buying lawn care customers, clubs & organizations, coupons & gift cards, co-marketing, door hangers, going door to door, flyers, internet marketing, lawn signs, customer letters, direct mailing, newsletters, newspaper ad, phone book advertising, phones & telemarketing, postcards, referrals, sports, testimonials, trade shows, truck & trailer advertising, word of mouth.

The Big Lawn Care Marketing Book
This book contains 470 pages of marketing ideas to help your lawn care & landscaping business grow.
The Big Lawn Care Marketing Book contains volume 1 & 2 of my other books "How to get customers for your landscaping and lawn care business all year long."

The landscaping and lawn care business plan startup guide.

If you ever had thought about starting your own lawn care or landscaping business but weren't sure how to go about putting together a business plan, this book will show you examples of lawn care business plans created on the Gopher Lawn Care Business Forum.

Inside is a step by step guide on how to make a landscape or lawn care business plan with real life examples including income and expense projections as well as customer acquisition goals. This lawn care business book is a great tool to help you improve your odds of finding success.

How to use Gopher Lawn Care Business Billing & Scheduling Software.

Learn how to manage your lawn care and landscaping business easier with this powerful software.

A Rebellious Teenagers Guide To Starting A Landscaping & Lawn Care Business.

When you are a teenager you have a lot of rebellious energy. Why not take that energy, harness it to be productive, and make money! This book will show you how to succeed in starting your own landscaping & lawn care business. I cover the basics of how to register your business to advanced topics like incentives to get employees to sell more.

GopherHaul Extreme Lawn Care Business Tips.

Unfiltered, unedited, and a little rough. A collection of landscaping & lawn care business lessons I've learned along the way.

I see so many new lawn care businesses get started only to fail a short time later because the entrepreneurs didn't educate themselves enough about their field. Here is a collection of lessons I learned that will give your lawn care or landscaping business a better chance at success.

**Lawn Care Business Tips, Tricks, & Secrets From The Gopher Lawn Care Business Forum & The GopherHaul Lawn Care Business Show.**
The vast majority of new lawn care businesses fail simply because they don't know the tips, tricks, and secrets veteran lawn care business owners have learned through years of trial and error. This book will share with you what you need to know.

**The GopherHaul guide on how to get customers for your landscaping and lawn care business - Volume 3.**
Coming up with marketing and service ideas to keep busy and profitable all year long can be difficult. Most of the times we are just not in the mood to sit and think up creative ways to make more money.
Well thankfully I have been able to interview thousands of lawn care business owners over the years and ask them what's worked and what hasn't. The responses and the follow up questions have really uncovered a treasure trove of ideas that I compiled here to share with you.

Now you don't have to get frustrated when trying to come up with new ideas. Just keep this book around as a reference. Some of these ideas might just work right off the shelf while others might need to be altered to fit your needs. Ultimately it's always better to have ideas on stand by just in case.

This book is the third in a series of lawn care business marketing books I have published and contains lawn care marketing ideas cherry picked from previous content I have written as well as new unpublished material.

 **How to Make More Money with your lawn care or landscaping business. From The Gopher Lawn Care Business Forum & The GopherHaul Lawn Care Business Show.**

Learn how to make more money with your lawn care or landscaping business.

Making money with your lawn care or landscaping business can be a challenge even in the best of times but it gets even tougher when you are up against heavy competition.

This book will help teach you what successful lawn care & landscaping business owners are doing to not only survive but to make more money than their competitors.

It covers how to make more money on bidding. How to read your customer's body language to know when you are charging too much or not enough. Learn the steps you should be taking to win more bids and things you should never do when trying to win a lawn care bid.

You will also learn how to deal with picky customers, those that live out of state, those that like to cancel service without giving you enough warning, and help you figure out how much your customers are actually worth.

Learn how to make more money with your lawn care crew by knowing the ideal crew size from others who have experimented with many different setups.

Learn the best way to purchase equipment, which equipment to purchase and how to use it in order to make your business more profitable plus much much more.

CUSTOMERS

Creating a new lawn care customer Welcoming Kit.

Are you giving all of your new lawn care customers a Welcoming Kit? If you aren't, you should start doing it. This is something that can really help keep your customers from leaving you and improve customer retention.

Here are some things to include in your lawn care customer Welcoming Kit folder.

- Welcoming letter.
- Newsletter.
- Business card.
- Mission statement.
- A list of your Frequently Asked Questions.
- List all the services you offer.
- A brochure on each major program you offer, like plant health care and bug barricade.
- Information on the supplementals you are currently promoting.
- A referral card to pass on to friends or family.

One lawn care business owner added "I started these welcome kits to help the new lawn care customers understand who we are and what we have to offer. When researching our cancellation history I found that most of the canceled lawn care accounts had been canceled within the first 3-4 months. If they had been more informed from the beginning, maybe we could have saved the sale. So this just goes to show you the importance of passing on this information to your new customers in the format of a Welcome Kit."

Lawn care customer retention. Why are your customers leaving you?

There are lawn care businesses that like to market their cheap price as their greatest strength. This tends to happen more frequently with newer businesses than those who have been around for a while. Being the cheapest lawn care service around is one of the fastest ways to go out of business. A big problem with cheap customers is a lack of customer retention. Why? Because they are always looking for the next cheapest deal.

One lawn care business owner wrote "I am always getting new customers, but then I will lose one. There seems to be a big turnover all the time. Is this how it is in the lawn biz? Just wondering if this is normal or am I doing something wrong.

These customers are not just one time cleanups calls either, they are for weekly lawn care, both residential and commercial.

At times, I think that I'm offering my service too cheap for the amount of work that I'm putting in for my clients. When I am on the job site, I always find myself doing an extra small job for every client to improve their yard. Nine times out of ten I'm not charging anything for that extra work. I was talking to another lawn care business owner, and he was telling me that I'm not charging enough. He would charge a lot more than what I'm changing for the average lawn."

A second lawn care business owner shared "there could be many factors involved with this customer churn. Is it possible other lawn care businesses are coming in and under bidding you? Could the customer be upset with your service? When your customers leave, do you ask them why? If so what are they saying? Also do you use yearly maintenance agreements? If not, have you considered using them in the future?

It could also be your customers are leaving because they're having a hard time equating the cost you're charging with the value they're receiving. As a result, when someone else comes along with a cheaper price (and lesser service), they drop you like an old boyfriend.

The key to success is to make sure they understand the VALUE they're receiving as a result of your service. It could be the extra attention you pay to their yard, or the years of experience you have in the industry, or the fact that you're licensed and insured. Each of these facts translates into some benefit for your customer and it's your job to make sure they understand what that benefit is.

Also, even though this may cause some debate among lawn care business owners, I firmly believe it's vital that you establish a relationship with your customers. Get to know them beyond the services you provide and take an interest in their lives. That doesn't mean invite yourself over for dinner, but consider sending them a monthly newsletter, birthday or holiday card. Call them periodically to check on things, etc.

Go that extra step to make them feel important and the next time a cheaper offer comes along, they'll think long and hard about dropping you.

You may be wondering how a business owner goes about asking customers who are leaving why they are leaving, should they ask if it is because of a lack of value?

How should they ask such a question? Should it just be simply, do you not feel you are getting enough value? And then should there be any follow ups to that like maybe so they can find out in what area they don't feel they are receiving value?

Ultimately you probably wouldn't need to ask if they're getting enough 'value', but simply asking them why they're leaving should give plenty of insight. If they say they're leaving because they found someone cheaper, that basically means they didn't feel as if they were getting enough value.

Value can be defined as what your customer gets for the price they pay. So it stands to reason that if they're leaving for someone that offers it cheaper, they're not getting enough value.

If that is indeed the case, it's time to examine the way you're positioning your service. It might also indicate a need to better educate your customers on your services and why you are a better choice than the neighborhood low ball scrub.

But again, you'll never know why they're leaving unless you ask the question.

You also have to consider you just might have the wrong type of customers and it has nothing to do with you. Perhaps because of how low your price is you are attracting the price shoppers.

Raise up your price and don't be disappointed that when customers tell you that you're too much. Don't expect to land every single account. If you do land every account, then 'yes' your prices are definitely too low."

How to improve your lawn care customer retention rates.

Every year a lawn care company is in business they will see their customer list recede a certain percentage. They may lose customers for many many reasons but one thing is for certain, each lawn care company will have a specific customer retention rate. That is the percentage of how many customers they have this year compare to last year. It's important to have a high customer retention rate because it can cost ten times more to generate a new lawn care customer than it does to maintain an existing customer. As we will see, if you focus on a certain type of customer, you can improve your retention rates.

I asked members of the Gopher Lawn Care Business Forum what their lawn care customer retention rate was and how they maintained it. Many had very insightful answers. Compare and contrast your lawn care customer retention rate with theirs and see if you can pick up some ideas to improve upon it.

What is your companies retention rate each year?

- "We have about a 75% - 85% retention rate."

- "For our monthly clients it's about a 90% retention for weekly and bi-weekly its about 50% retention.

I categorize my customer base in this manner. I find that weekly customers are people who want work done every week but then cut your neck in the winter. Bi-weekly customers are every other week in the growing season and then drop you during the winter. Monthly are clients that pay a set fee all 12 months. When I give a bid I try to steer them all to become monthly through price. Like $100 a month, $30 a visit, $35 every other week.

If a client wants any thing but monthly they are probably trying to save money. I also don't give them the same level of service that a monthly lawn care customer gets. You know in most cases as soon as the grass stops growing, then they don't pay and I don't allow people to call me a month later for service just so they can save a buck. If you wait that long my view is you need to find another lawn care service provider."

- "I haven't checked mine for sure but those numbers seem like I would be pretty close to them. I think monthly customers who are willing to sign a lawn care contract, want long term service right from the get go, so it's easy. They are not going to do it themselves, so show up as scheduled & keep them happy and they will stay with you.

Weekly per cut clients often want services on weird schedules so I tend to stick to my guns with them. Through the growing season I service weekly customers at price 'A' and bi-weekly at price 'B' (on set scheduled days). I don't play the 'we'll call you when we want you to come out game' & I'm not calling them every week to see if it's Ok to come today and mow their lawn. So I tend to drop those clients. Some others only want service for short periods of time like say the really hot months & that's fine. I've found ways to get even those customers to call me back next year.

The weekly people come & go more often that's why I prefer monthly clients. It's an ongoing relationship month in, month out, season in & season out. You are their landscaper. I find it easier to maintain a healthy relationship with my annual (monthly) clients."

- "My view is with price comes a value. With value comes a price.

I am the most expensive guy on the block and I have a 95% client retention rate. What I offer my clients is what they pay for and more.

I had another lawn care company go to every one of my clients with an ad stating that they would offer a quote 10% lower than their current provider. I had clients calling me telling me that this company was doing this cutthroat approach. So I asked those customers why they called and why they would not switch? They said that they expect to pay more for the level of service I provide."

- "Last year our level of business grew as the season progressed. It had us kind of scrambling to get it all done all season long. I inherited some accounts, from a previous owner, at the beginning of the season and they were woefully under priced in my opinion. I raised prices considerably across the board, but to help alleviate the sticker shock I offered the fifth mow and tenth mow free. I now, this year, have prices where they needed to be and my customer base is used to paying these prices. Retention rate is at or above 99% as well with our only lost account coming from an elderly woman selling her house and moving away."

As you can see many lawn care business owners find they can improve their lawn care customer retention rates by servicing customers who are willing to sign up for an annual contract and are not looking to price shop. Consider this as a way to screen new potential customers when they call and improve your customer retention rates.

Commercial lawn care customer won't sign a contract?

Think before you act. That is one lesson you should pull from this discussion on the Gopher Lawn Care Business Forum. Here a lawn care business owner is given the opportunity to perform lawn care services for a large warehouse. The downside to the job is that the customer won't sign any contracts. As you read through this, you will see the pros and cons to working with such a lawn care customer and it may help you in figuring out which is the best way to go and why.

He wrote "I just made a great contact with a new commercial lawn care customer. It's a warehouse. They want weekly lawn cuts during the growing season (April-September), then it will slow to 3 cuts per month for March and October. During the winter they want 2 cuts per month from November to February.

They also want edging of all hard surfaces and weed eating to be performed every 2 weeks during the growing season and as needed during the off-season. Clippings and other debris to be blown from walks, patios, and parking areas after each mowing. Plant beds to be weeded by chemical means and supplemented by hand. Weeding is to be performed once a month to provide a weed free environment. All trees and shrubs to be pruned 2 times a year at the appropriate time for plant and flower developments using proper horticultural practices. Pine straw will be put out 2 times a year(April/October) at the appropriate time.

I called them on the phone and asked about having them sign a lawn care contract and they said they don't do contracts. It's a 30 day pay term. If you don't do a good job, then you are fired. If you do good work you can stay for another 20 days and so on and so on. Their previous lawn care operator supposedly did a terrible job and they don't want to get burned again.

Does this sound like a good idea or should I cut and run?"

A second lawn care business owner said "this job is throwing up red flags everywhere. It's not worth the trouble. At any time they can say ok we don't want to use you anymore and you're gone, all while they are holding 30 days worth of work and unpaid invoices.

The only thing you might be able to try for is a month to month contract, and that is risky at best. I wouldn't touch any commercial lawn care work without a contract. They like to hold onto the money for as long as they can get away with.

A contract is a legal binder between 2 or more parties. I have done things like this before and got more headaches than pay.

Please know this, to some I may sound hard and I'm only about the money well I am. We are in business to make money and provide a lawn care landscape service. We are not a collection service. Collections cost you money even if you get paid collecting late fees and other fees. It still costs you money. You have to know when to walk away, and this one I would walk away from, it just isn't worth the time.

Weigh the pro's and con's. If the pro's out weigh the cons then go for it. You really need to sit down and name five real good things that would benefit your company by taking this job. I personally would walk on this one."

A third lawn care business owner said "Why not put in a bid? Remember, we are businessmen and business is all about negotiation.

Too often, lawn care business owners think that they have to accept whatever contract is offered. You have every right to write your own demands into a contract.

Don't be intimidated just because it is a big warehouse. If they want to give you month-by-month work it is probably because their last lawn care business did a poor job. Don't be like that last guy. Prove yourself and make them trust you.

If I were going to have a month-by-month agreement, I would write into my proposal that I want payment on the 30th of the same month I do the work or get paid per job. I would want one NAMED supervisor to interact with and approve my work and he will sign a P.O. or a satisfaction form at each visit (or once per month). I also want the ability to cease working for them on a month-by-month basis (if they like your work, they will transfer you to a yearly contract in no time).

Speak with the supervisor who will approve your work. If you feel comfortable with him and if you are in full understanding with the work to be done, by all means, bid accordingly.

Never low-ball a bid like this. If they want quality work, they should be willing to pay for it. Speak with the supervisor to let him know you charge more because you take extra time to make sure everything it done correctly.

If they don't agree with your proposal, walk away.

I have done tons of work with factories and industrial complexes like this. I have always found starting out on the right foot with great communication is the key when working with the supervisors. They are normally very amiable.

Once you get in, it is fairly easy to talk them into additional work such as building planters around their driveway entrances to make the area look better.

When the company's vice presidents are scheduled to pay them a visit, they will often call you for a 'RUSH' job to which you can say 'I can do it today but I need an extra $100 to adjust my schedule.'

I know some lawn care business owners that don't like this type of work but I always found it to be some of the best money around. Once your foot is in the door and they see you provide high quality work, you should have an easy time with it."

Dealing with pain in the ass customers.

A member of the Gopher lawn Care Business Forum had just posted about how he won his bid for mowing a large commercial property. This new commercial lawn care job is really going to help his business grow next year. And I asked him:

When you read some of the post on this forum and see some lawn care business owners have such a difficult time getting their footing in this business, do you feel they are missing something? What do you feel has gotten you to the next level when so many fail at even getting a footing? What are others simply not doing?

He wrote "I think you have to have a solid business plan and set goals for your business. I decided to build my business around personal service. I build relationships with my clients. This has led to many long time accounts as well as lots of 'word of mouth' clients. There are a lot of the larger landscape company's that don't cater to personal service. I here it all the time. I will do little things for my customers that don't take a lot of time like carry in patio furniture, or garden hoses, I even hung some pictures for one of my clients. You also have to be able to sell yourself and your services. Knowledge is definitely key.

My advice to new startups in this business is to have a plan to set yourself apart from the competition. Don't try to be like every other lawn boy running around out there just trying to cut grass and rake leaves."

Having a business plan seems to be really important! The tough thing about it is that it doesn't happen over night. You can't print a flyer, drop it off and then immediately be known for personal service.

How long do you think it took you to start getting to the point where your personal service really took center stage?

Also, how did you come up with the idea that personal service would be your niche? It's genius and simple and 99% of the time, overlooked. I just wonder how this idea stood out for you?

"It took a couple years and a number of customers for me to realize that there is a niche for personal service. First off I want clients that I enjoy servicing. That makes going to work much more fun. I have weeded out the PITA (pain in the ass) clients.

When you go above and beyond in your service, most people take notice and appreciate that. That has brought us more business thru referrals than any flyer or newspaper ads ever did."

That is a very interesting point. A lot of new business owners will have no clue about this.

What, to you, defines a pain in the ass customer? When does a customer go from being demanding to being a pita? What are the signs you look out for?

Once they get that category, how do you get rid of them?

"To me a PITA customer is someone who you just can't please no matter how hard you try or someone who expects more than what we agreed upon.

For example:

Early last spring we had this new client that wanted her lawn mowed at like 3 different heights depending on which side of the house you were on. She would call 3 times a week if she saw 1 dandelion on her lawn. I told her we would take care of the dandelion when we show up for her next weekly mowing. She demanded that we return within a day to remove it. 1 dandelion not a patch of them!

Needless to say after 3 weeks of that crap I terminated her services. That type of client is not who I want to work for after all this is my business! A PITA client could be someone who doesn't pay on time as well. I don't use contracts for residential customers. For commercial customers, I put an escape clause in the contract for me and the customer. That way if things don't work out, they or we, are not locked in for the entire season.

Commercial clients like the escape clause because some of them have been burned by shoddy workmanship especially from the large landscape company's which will only sign a contract for the entire season."

Very fascinating, so maybe the key to enjoying your company and growing it is finding the customers you work best with. You can't make everyone happy all the time but you can make some of the people happy some of the time. Finding a customer you feel you can make happy seems to be an important goal. For those you can't make happy, cut them free and move on.

Make your jobs smoother by involving the lawn care client.

To some lawn care business owners, the client has two jobs. One is to accept the bid and the other is to approve the finished project and make payment. Between those two points they may not want to hear anything from the client at all. But as we have seen on the Gopher Lawn Care Business Forum, the more you involve the client, the smoother you can make the job go. This comes in especially handy when you run into a problem onsite and you need the customer to hold it together and not fly off the handle.

Here is a great example of this, a member wrote "I did a drain job this week by myself as we are short staff, it was one of the worst yet as the clay content was, well like cement.

I had the rock dumped in the clients driveway while I transported it with the tractor, the client didn't have access to their front stairs for a while but this customer wanted to get some coffee. I offer to give her a ride up to the back of the house on my tractor, as it was raining and the front bank is very steep, she loved it.

This is one of those jobs that could have gone south fast, due to it being so wet and the heavy clay. It made a major mess of their side and back yard, I involved them as much as possible and everything worked out and they understood. The staff finished sodding yesterday and they wrote saying they are very happy, have to drop down today for payment and see the job."

That was a very creative and fun way to get the customer involved on the job site and to show that you care about your interaction with them. How do you feel this interaction effected their attitude towards you and the job?

"How did this change the client's attitude? This was morning two. The back yard was a mess and she has quite a temper and use of the English language. It seemed after this she was really cool and even came out to help. I found things that I could get her to do and praised her work, in the end everyone was happy.

I went by today for payment and they offered me to stay for lunch which I did, everyone is pleased with the results. Don't think this only applies to residential customers. This was just my most recent example of involving the customer on a jobsite. I work just as close with my commercial clients as well and recommend you do too."

Not enough lawn care liability insurance? Customer might not pay!

There are so many things that go on in life where you just wish you knew something was going to become a problem, before you got into it. To help you take one of those unknowns off your list, let's look at this story. Did you know commercial lawn care customers might withhold payment unless you can prove you have the proper liability insurance level? Read on....

One lawn care business owner shared a story about a situation he ran into and wrote "I just called my insurance company to find out some information on coverage for my lawn care business and learned something I never knew before.

As I am taking the jump from residential to commercial lawn care customers, I am learning how much of a pain in the ass a commercial contract can be. Because of a situation I currently find myself in, I am now learning how a commercial customer can withhold payment until you are able to provide proof you have their mandated level of liability insurance.

My insurance agent is confirming this happens to others and told me they get a lot of contractors who get commercial contracts, and go ahead and do the job. Once completed, the customer withholds payment and says 'well, you don't have enough liability coverage, so we're not going to pay you until you get the correct coverage.'

At that point you're stuck with no payment and have to get the coverage they require. If you are broke and can't afford insurance or can't afford to spend more to get the proper amount of insurance at the time, you can really find yourself in a bad spot. My advice to you is to not leave any of this to chance. Don't be in such a rush that that you take a commercial lawn care job without knowing this ahead of time. Get your agreement with the commercial customer it in writing before any jobs are started and make sure your company has enough coverage."

A second lawn care business owner added, "people play all kind of games, especially when they think they can get away with it. Commercial lawn care customers will at times have cash flow problems just like everyone else and do things to try to delay payment. Withholding payment due to lack of insurance may be an angle they try to use to put off writing a check for a period of time. It could also be a method they chose to force you to purchase the proper liability insurance coverage that protects you as well as them.

In general, it's best to avoid problems in advance. That is why I supply all commercial lawn care customers with my certificate of insurance at the time of my bid. Most commercial properties will provide you with a bid sheet that states how much liability insurance you will need to bid, along with what work they are requiring to be completed."

Watch out for goofy commercial lawn care contracts.

Anyone can create a lawn care contract. All you need to do is put pen to paper and write whatever it is floating around in your head. Then when you are asked to sign it, no matter how goofy it is, if you do sign it, you are agreeing to it. So think before you sign any contract. What may seem at first glance to be a great property to service. One that is going to bring you a lot of money, can take a dark turn when a bad lawn care contract is presented for you to sign. Things can go from great to rotten in a matter of minutes.

Let's take a look at such a situation that caused a lawn care business owner on the Gopher Lawn Care Business Forum to take a step back and think twice about before taking the job.

He wrote "I have a large project to bid on with six properties in my area. The property manager sent me a lawn care maintenance contract and some of the language used seems a little off to me. Here is what he wants me to sign.

Landscape Maintenance Agreement:

_____agrees to provide the services necessary to achieve and maintain high quality care and "curb appeal" as described below, for the landscaping of the six facilities owned by _____.

In exchange for these services, _____ agrees to pay a maximum of _____per month plus tax. This is an annually reviewed "at will" contract which may be ended by either party with 30 days notice.

• This service includes all treatments such as fertilizing, weed

killers and other landscape chemicals.
• All sites will be mowed, edged, Weed whacked and reseeded as needed
• Curb appeal as defined by _____ will be improved and maintained at all sites
• All plant beds will be weeded cleaned and raked as needed
• All sidewalks and driveways will be kept free of debris as needed
• All building roofs and asphalt areas will be cleaned of moss and maintained as needed using moss killer and pressure washer.
• All branches will be trimmed and kept off security fences, buildings and driveways as needed
• All shrubbery, bushes plants and small trees will be pruned as needed with dead plants being removed and disposed of
• All gutters will be kept clean and free of debris at all times
• Leaves will be gathered and removed and flowers will be watered as needed
• All landscape debris will be removed and disposed of by contractor daily.
• Light snow removal and application of de-icer will be done as required
• Bark and gravel will be supplied and applied at $25 per yard at the request of the main office of ____
• Contractor will provide a weekly work order form for the site manager to sign off on in order to ensure that the work is being completed as agreed
• Contractor agrees to a weekly schedule at each site rain or shine informing management of any schedule changes

_____ _____

Does this seem to be a normal contract? How will I remove and dispose of debris daily? Should I amend the contract?"

A second lawn care business owner said "having spent over 14 years in this business with a good working knowledge of what we do in the lawn care industry, I personally have some concerns with the contract as you posted it. I am not a lawyer but have been involved with hundreds of contracts. Let's take a look at your contract piece by piece and analyze it.

pay a maximum of _____ per month plus tax.

The word Maximum is not a defined term in the context of the agreement, as such I would suggest it be removed and the property manager pay a set price per month.

high quality care and "curb appeal"

Well this is pretty open, curb side appeal to me may not be curb side appeal to the customer, define it.

weed killers and other landscape chemicals.

Chemicals are not allowed in our city. I would have this changed to weed control. Who is responsible if you use a product in good faith and then it does damage, i.e. who is on the hook? You because you agreed or the owner because you were instructed to.

Curb appeal as defined by _____ will be improved and maintained at all sites

Where is it defined?

All sidewalks and driveways will be kept free of debris as needed

Who defines the need? Is it daily, every few days, as called etc.

I see all kinds of warning signals and an agreement that was written by an amateur with probably good intentions but you are leaving yourself wide open.

Instead why not write a contract that defines what you will do and what you will do for each service and how often, this one is not clear at all.

It seems like this company has probably been burnt in the past and may have hacked together this contract to try and remedy the situation. I think that is why you see it's 'at will'. They want to be able to get out of it if they are not happy. Why not just say look, here is what I think your property needs, here is the monthly price and let's go from there.

Are you getting a weird vibe from them already from other things besides the contract? Have you asked them if they have had any problems with previous lawn care businesses and if so, what were the problems? The more you know, the better you can fix the situation.

He responded and said "basically I wrote the property manager back with a new contract. I actually used one of the lawn care contract templates from the Gopher Forum. I put my company name in and told him that I felt we needed to write up a new lawn care contract that was more quantifiable for the 'as needed' parts. I am hoping he just has been burned in the past or doesn't really have a clue and my new contract will clarify things for the both of us.

But now that I am the wiser, I won't be signing the contract they presented."

What if you miss a potential lawn care customer's call?

When you are just getting your lawn care business started, missing a potential new lawn care customer's phone call is a big deal. It's a big deal when you have been in business for a while too, but it seems especially important when you are just getting started which leads me to this great question that was asked on the Gopher Lawn Care Business Forum.

A new lawn care business owner wrote "I just started my own lawn care business and passed out flyers earlier today. Later in the day, while at my baseball game, someone called wanting lawn service. I called him back right away but, I got his answering machine. The bad news is that his mailbox was full. It gave me the option to page him so I did that. So far, he hasn't called back. When he left me his initial message he also gave me his address. He lives in the same neighborhood as me. My question is, should I walk down to his house and talk to him since I can't get a hold of him by phone."

Such a great question and one that many new lawn care business owners will run into. Here are some equally insightful responses that should help you.

One member said "face to face is always the best sales approach. He called you so you are not cold calling. Showing up at his door shows your character and professionalism."

Another added "If I miss a call, I usually call back. If there is no answer, I search their home address online through their phone number. Then I will drive by their home just to make sure I even want to deal with them. They might have grass up to my neck, or some other problem. If that's the case I'll avoid the call.

Otherwise if there is no problem with the lawn, I will knock on the door. If they aren't home I will write my estimate on the back of my business card & stick it where they can see it, or in the mail box. Then I will call later to confirm if they had received my card & if they had any questions."

One last business owners shared their view by saying "an opportunity missed is an opportunity lost. Without a doubt, go pay him a visit and if he/she is not home, leave a note saying thanks for your call, I tried to call you however your mail box is full, would love to discuss your lawn care needs, please call me at.."

So I hope you can see from this discussion the importance of following up on missed phone calls. It's simple steps like these that can make the difference between a business succeeding or not.

When should your lawn care business send thank you letters?

Reaching out to your lawn care customers and letting them know they are appreciated is very important. This is all too often overlooked because the average lawn care business owner is just simply overwhelmed with the day to day activities of running the business. As a small business owner, you have many great opportunities to reach out to your customers and this leads me to a question asked a on the Gopher Lawn Care Business Forum.

One lawn care business owner wrote "when should a lawn care business send thank you letters to customers?"

A second business owner shared "the thank you letter is an important and often overlooked aspect of making your lawn care customers feel appreciated.

Thank you notes or letters can be delivered at anytime. For example:

- After a signing a new customer to a maintenance agreement.
- At the end of a season.
- After signing or completing a big job.
- After they have referred someone else to your company.
- Anytime you want to thank your customer or just remind them that you are still here.

Thank you notes should be brief and to the point. Consider a card or postcard to say thanks. The note may be accompanied by a small gift in special circumstances however do not include marketing material. It would seem like you are trying to sell them something under the pretense of doing something nice. The purpose of the thank you note is to do a nice thing for the sake of doing it so leave out the flyers or other advertisements. That being said there is nothing wrong with following up after a couple of weeks with some promotional material.

The above information relates to a specific thank you note however always remember to thank your customers for their business in all of your correspondence to them.

With all of this in mind, go out and get printed up some lawn care business thank you cards and the next time these opportunities present themselves where you can make the customer feel appreciated, jump on it!"

MARKETING METHODS

How many welcome letters should each lawn care customer get?

I am constantly learning new things on the Gopher Lawn Care Business Forum. The things that amaze me the most are the things that I just would have never thought of without the help of others. Take for example this simple topic. How many welcome letters should you send to each of your new lawn care customers? I would figure one would suffice. However, when we started talking about it, I learned that other lawn care business owners were sending up to FOUR! Four welcome letters at different times to a new customer! Who would have thunk!

Initially I was talking about a concept where each new lawn care customer would get a letter specific to their needs. However as we got into this the discussion grew and taught me as your lawn care business grows, so does your need to change your marketing. As your client list grows longer, you are probably going to have less time to spend on each customer individually which leads to having less time to customize your marketing for each client. Instead, you will find a need to create more generic marketing material that can be used for all of your new customers.

One lawn care business owner wrote "our company is too big to customize our marketing. With 15 lawn care technicians and an average of 25 lawns per technician, it would be difficult to keep track of them all.

I think making sure the customer is well informed on how your company handles different situations would help with the customer retention. In my welcome kit, I have tried to include answers to every question they may have."

Do you mean you include a general list of business frequently asked questions? Like who to contact. How you bill etc. Or do you mean more like lawn specific problem questions?

"Both. It contains the frequently ask questions about how we do business & answers about how much the lawn should be watered, mowed, etc. Also answers about what to do after the fertilization applications, and if they come across any problems with their lawns.

Sending a personalized letter with specifics about the property can be very beneficial, but at the same time it's almost too much work for the return you would get on that work.

When your company gets bigger you want to create marketing materials that are reusable and duplicatible. So for instance, early on when our business got started, we sent letters to customers that showed before and after pictures of each customer's lawn to show how we have improved it. Now instead of taking Before & After shots of each particular customers lawn, we use a picture of a generic lawn we've done previously to convey the story we want to get across.

We also send a few 'welcome' letters.

- One immediately after they sign the contract.
- Another before the first service visit, this could be in your 'Welcome Kit'.
- Another immediately after the first lawn care service visit.
- And then another one a week later.

Each one would contain something different that cements the relationship, reminds the customer of all the benefits they'll be receiving, and potentially even upsells or lets them know about additional services we offer as well.

Ultimately, it comes down to building a relationship with the customer and viewing them like a person, not a transaction. The instant they become simply a transaction is the instant they're on their way out the door as a customer. Especially in today's economy.

Another key piece to retaining your customers is to make sure they are happy with the services you are performing. By sending them a survey to see if we have met their expectations so far, or to see if they have any questions we may be able to answer, can help build our bond with the customer even further.

To come up with a list of frequently asked questions, for your welcome kit I suggest sitting down and making a list of general questions you hear from your customers. Ideally they're ones that come up frequently, but it could also include questions that we might think are extremely basic.

One thing to remember is that it's easy to assume people know the basics about what you do. In most cases however, people don't have the first idea so my rule of thumb is never assume anything.

So the next time you sign up a new lawn care customer, you will be well equipped to do the best you can to retain that customer for the long haul and make them feel appreciated and wanted."

A free marketing method to get more lawn care customers.

You can never have enough marketing ideas written down to experiment with. As you try them, you will find some work well for you while others may not. Continue your marketing experimentation with the ones you find that work. Change one variable about them and try again. See if you get better or worse results because of that change. Keep this cycle going and you will find real killer marketing techniques.

A veteran lawn care business owner, shared with us one of his big lawn care marketing secrets on the Gopher Lawn Care Business Forum that you may want to add to your list of marketing ideas. He wrote "I have been running my lawn care and landscaping service now for about 8 years and have tried many things to get new customers. Not all have worked, but here is one that has.

I have found this marketing idea to generate a ton of business for me and it cost nothing at all !! First what I do is I drive around my town or city and I pick up as many real estate magazines as I find. They are usually outside restaurants, shopping malls etc. They will be in little boxes marked Free real estate magazines. I then go through all the magazines and write down the email addresses to as many realtors as I see in there. You will find them inside the magazines on each realtor's advertisement.

Next I go into word or my email program and write a short but sweet message. I try to keep it between 5 to 7 sentences. The message will discuss how I can save the realtor money this upcoming year and keep there properties ready to sell at all times by using my awesome lawn care business !! I save the body of the email and just go in and change the name each time I send it to a different realtor.

Depending on the number of contacts you find, this will take a few hours to pull off but I think it's well worth it and it cost me nothing to do.

I have found I get a ton of business of doing this one marketing technique alone. Sometimes I get lucky and get in with a BIG realtors that sells millions per year. With such realtors, you can stay super busy off this one account alone.

I have one realtor I have been working with for years now and just off of her account alone I got 12 new houses and some commercial buildings as well. All for free and all from one simple email! That's how it started with me and it's been growing ever since.

Another great idea is to do this same marketing strategy but target PROPERTY MANAGEMENT COMPANIES in your city or town. They manage properties for other people and owners (homes, apartments, rental property, office buildings, manufacturing plants etc). Do the same steps as above and watch the business come in !!"

12 steps to get more commercial lawn care customers.

One of the biggest questions we see on the Gopher Lawn Care Business Forum is about getting new customers. There are some techniques that are similar between getting commercial and residential customers but there are some techniques that differ as well. Here is a list of 12 steps your lawn care business should consider taking in order to improve your chances of landing more commercial lawn care clients.

One lawn care business owner wrote "I found for our company that the best way to approach commercial lawn care accounts is with persistence and lots of patience. Here are 12 steps you can take to improve your ability to gain commercial lawn care accounts.

1. Create your company portfolio. This should include pictures, letters, insurance and so on.

2. Grab a phone book or google the property management companies in your area of business.

3. Go and visit those on your list and hand out your portfolio and ask to be put on there bidding list.

4. Make sure that each manager get's a portfolio and you get a business card from them.

5. Wait for a couple of weeks and either email them or call them asking if there's any properties available that you can bid on. Don't be pushy or try to over sell yourself.

6. When they start to give you jobs to bid on, do not, I repeat do

not, guess on pricing. Get your surveyor's wheel out and measure the property. Then use the lawn care estimator calculators on the Gopher Forum. You'll be surprised to know that when guessing a property even though you might be close on your man hours, you'll lose money on your fert, mulch etc.

7. When dealing with a property management company, never say 'I Don't Know.' If you don't have an answer for them, tell them their question is noted and you'll email them a reply or get back to them.

8. Get the property manager to rely on you as much as possible. My goal is to do their job for them. I have a few managers that instead of performing weekly visits, they visit the property once a month or longer to inspect it. I manage the property and they've come to rely on me for it. So when you got a bid out, they'll be the first one's telling the board members that you're the best thing since slice bread.

9. Get to know the board members if your in a community with board members. Property management companies come and go but most of the time, board members stay longer and have the final say.

10. Return calls ASAP even if it's just to tell them that your busy and will call them back later.

11. Give back to the community. I've budgeted 20, 3 gallon plants per year that I can plant for free, if need be, I use it. When I bill them and include a freebie extra, I let them know it's at no charge.

12. When doing a walk through, don't point out things you see wrong. Let them do all the talking if possible. Only acknowledge what's being said and take care of it.

Don't waste my time giving out unsolicited lawn care bids. For me it's a tacky way of trying to generate business. With the portfolio, it's all out there. It saves you the time of measuring out a property, just to have it tossed in the trash, also what if you come in at a higher price? For me there's too much negative in doing it that way.

There are a few other things but I found this list includes the most personal & cost effective methods for our company to operate. The bidding process is like filling out a job application and like a job application most of the time (more than not) it gets filed in the TB (Trash Bin) and you're forgotten.

With the way I handle getting new commercial lawn care clients, I've got management companies calling me out of the wood work and all I did was introduce my company & myself to them years ago letting them know that I'm here when they need me. Heck I've got a management company that only calls me to bail them out. We've even gone as far as walking properties with them and pointing out what we saw wrong in order to help them (managers) manage the other lawn care companies that are dropping the ball.

So try these techniques out and I am sure they will improve your ability to land more commercial lawn care clients."

Using inside contacts to land commercial lawn care bid.

Marketing to your social network is a great way to find new lawn care jobs. All too often, new lawn care business owners spend a ton of money trying to reach out to people they don't know when they could spend a lot less to gain customers from people they do know. Here is a great example of that from a discussion on the Gopher Lawn Care Business Forum.

One lawn care business owner wrote "I am just starting up a small lawn care business around my neighborhood as a side job while I go to college. I'm studying to be an engineer and figured this would be a very flexible job considering I can make my own hours. I had cut lawns in the past when I was a little younger and made some good money as a high school student. This time around though, I am looking to take it to a higher level.

The other day, I got an insider tip about a local bid that is needed. I found out through my sister who is a member of a home owner's association board, that they are looking to replace their current lawn care service provider due to shoddy workmanship. She suggested that I submit a formal proposal to the HOA but I'm not entirely sure how to do that. I'd assume they would want grass cutting, edging, and small landscaping. This my first time submitting a commercial lawn care proposal so I am completely lost."

A second lawn care business owner suggested "with your sister being on the board it would be wrong for her to tell you what price they are shooting for. This would most likely be a violation of their convents and bylaws. Now on the other hand, being that your sister lives in the HOA neighborhood, she will receive a monthly, quarterly, bi yearly or yearly balance sheets or profit &

loss budget. You can visit her as a brother and ask to see those sheets and review them. Look for categories like landscape maintenance, irrigation repair/maintenance, fertilization/pest/weed control, tree trimming and mulch landscape. This will give you a break down of what the costs were for the association during those times.

Before you go about attempting to put together a proposal you should first ask and take a tour of the property with the president of the board. Find out the locations of every job that is going to be required of you. If you are behind houses, ask how close they expect you to cut to the owners property lines. If there are waterways or retention ponds, are you to mow to the water line and would you need to line trim around the entire water? Are you expected to replace dead or damaged sod at cost plus labor? In maintenance of the sprinkler system, do you run it monthly and fix what needs to be fixed or can you sub-contract that out? This can be a costly service and a great money maker.

How often and where will you have to mulch? Will they be requiring new mulch at entrance ways, parks, around trees, shrubs, beds, signs etc.? What about how often would you need to replant flowers/plants? How often to trim trees, remove dead limbs or whole trees? Would you need to plant annuals or perennials? Can you sub out fertilization as part of the proposal?

I have been burned by all this before when I was first making that jump to commercial customers so I have a better idea now where you can get stuck. You need to make sure that you are on the same page with the HOA and fully understand what is expected of you and what you expect from them. Also ask if there is a management company that helps the HOA. Networking with them could bring you more jobs in the future. Bring a note pad to take a lot of notes and a camera/video device to assist you in ensuring that you have it documented.

Be organized and look professional. You may not get the job but this will be a great experience for you. Be prepared and don't bite off more then you can chew. If it seems like too much for you to handle, walk away and go for smaller, more easily manageable lawn care accounts."

How to land restaurants and hotels as lawn care clients.

Any time I hear a great story on how a lawn care business owner landed some commercial accounts, I like to share the story with everyone to help you see how others do it. We all need to hear stories and experiences from others in order to broaden our horizons. This story came to us through the Gopher Lawn Care Business Forum where a member shared with us how he landed 4 hotels, 2 restaurants and 47 residential lawn care customers. Look at the way he did it and compare his operation with yours. Then ask yourself if there are areas in your business you could improve upon.

He wrote "I restarted my lawn service last year. I used to have about 12 yards in high school, but girls and the beach were way more important than cutting grass and my business failed because of it. After that experience I worked for a landscaping company through college. Later I worked as a regional manager for a cellular dealer for 9 years until that got old.

During that time I saved up some money and left that line of work to restart my lawn care business. I now have 4 hotels, 2 restaurants and 47 residential.

I got the 2 restaurants just by going up to the managers and asking them who is doing there lawn service (because it looked awful) and they said basically they didn't have anyone. I gave them a price and showed up the next day and started edging and mowing. It was that simple! So as you drive around town, keep your eyes open and don't be afraid to walk in the door and introduce yourself!

I got the 4 hotels from the signs on my landscaping truck &

trailer. The property manager for all 4 hotels called to get a estimate for his house. While speaking with him I told him I provided commercial lawn services as well. From there, he told me what he did and said he wasn't happy with his current landscaping company....so for about a month we went back and forth on prices and the only way to close the deal was to throw in his home's lawn service for free. His yard only takes 25 minutes to edge and mow, so there was no big loss there when compared to the profit I was making from the hotels. Once he said yes we sealed the deal.

Vehicle graphics are very important! I made the graphics for my trailer on my own computer and emailed them to a local sign & banner company. We decided to put them on the side of my truck for people to see when my trailer was off. I have the same sign on the back of my trailer also! This is such a simple step, every lawn care business should be doing this.

Next season this hotel company is opening up 2 more hotels and I also got the contract to mow those properties as well. Another marketing angle I utilize is reaching out to all the employees at each hotel. I was able to put up a flyer in their break room and send a flyer home with their pay check! Example: ABC Hotel employee get a 10% discount on yard service! This made the property manager look good and also got me more local residential lawn care accounts.

When I need more residential lawn care customers, I knock on doors that need bushes trimmed, mulching, mowing and edging done. This works great. While I am there I will offer my weekly or bi-weekly lawn care services. Once I get them as customers I ask for and start getting referrals."

Should you email market to real estate agents?

Email marketing is a real simple way of reaching out to new potential customers, but is it worthwhile? That is what one business owner questioned on the Gopher Lawn Care Business Forum. Interestingly enough, another lawn care business owner who is also a licensed real estate agent, responded with some insight that will surely help your business get a bigger bang for your marketing efforts.

He wrote "I need help coming up with a professional email to send to local realtors. I have already been in contact with realtors and handed out flyers and business cards to them, but I want to try and reach more through email.

What I have done so far is test e-mailed 12 realtors this week, offering them a free mowing. If they don't like the work we do no harm, no foul. But if they like it, they have the option of hiring us or referring us to others they know. So far I have gotten one response. The realtor said he doesn't choose the lawn care companies for his clients but he would refer me to them. Not very good results in my opinion.

That's all I've gotten so far out of talking to a few realtors and I am guessing those results are typical. But that single contact could still lead somewhere!! You gotta think positively!

I'm trying to pick up realtors to help with houses that are sitting on the market and potentially being passed on by the potential buyers. Mowing, trimming, and all the normal services will be offered. I also offer a free mow with a signed yearly lawn care agreement.

I am looking for more suggestions or ideas on how to handle this better."

A second lawn care business owner wrote "I'm a licensed real estate broker as well as operate my own lawn care business. After reading this, I do have some observations/suggestions to share.

First off, I would not email any real estate agent unless I already had a relationship with him/her. There are a few reasons for this. MANY agents will view these emails as spam. Secondly, many will think it's lazy marketing and be turned off by it. Thirdly many may not even get the email as it could get trapped in a spam folder.

Instead, here's what I'd do:

- Visit each local Real Estate office and ask to distribute flyers in the agent's mailboxes. Don't go with black and white printing, instead go with a professional looking color piece.
- Most offices have a weekly or monthly sales meeting. Offer to bring donuts (agents love food) and plenty of business cards & brochures to go along to a future meeting.
- Visit an agent at a model home or open house and speak with them ONLY if they are not busy and aren't interacting with customers at the moment.

If you live in a big metro area or small town, you'll obviously have to adjust your marketing plan of attack for the agents. In the past, I had dealt with one lawn care business owner that I'd call for mowing work on vacant houses with out of town sellers. The seller would OK the work/price and the mow guy would direct bill the seller. This business owner was kept very busy.

As far as other services, I did not have a list of people I'd use, but many realtors did, so I'd ask around. If the seller still lived in the same town, they'd usually handle the lawn care on their own, which brings up another marketing opportunity. Sellers may want to have someone take care of their yard as they're busy house shopping, packing, etc. Especially if they move out of town.

Here's another tip: Talking to realtors is good, but what I found to be BETTER and bring you FASTER results is to talk to the property management branch of whatever realty companies are in your area. In my area, for example, there are 3 major realtors who handle property management. Find the agents who specialize in this area, and present your business directly to these folks. I have done good with this, and I have held a $38,000 / year contract with one of them for 9 years now and running. You will be targeting shopping centers, office complexes, medical buildings, and multi-family units. Aim high and ask for more than you think you can handle. Really, if you land an account that's too big for your operation, take it and treat the customer with the same friendly attitude you would have as if you were sealing the deal on a $40.00 residential job. Don't get freaked out by the larger sized jobs. You will quickly get used to them and remember, people can sense when you are in over your head, if you let it show."

Going big come hell or high water with my lawn care marketing.

You'd be amazed how much business you could drum up if you put your mind to it. Most lawn care business owners tend to spend more time working on jobs than marketing. What if you stepped up your marketing effort a little more? If you did, where would you put that additional energy? Would you hand out a few more business cards? Maybe distribute a few more lawn care flyers?

A member of the Gopher Lawn Care Business Forum shared with us his aggressive lawn care marketing plan. You may want to compare your plan with his and see where you could improve. He wrote "this year I decided to go big, come hell or high water. I started aggressively marketing to residential and commercial customers. Because of the new contacts I made, I just recently had the opportunity to bid on 5 large apartments. These jobs will be very good money and could launch me into the six figure income range. I will hopefully be signing the contracts next week.

I am keeping all of my residential customers as I grow my commercial side. I will definitely have to hire some more help this year. I will also have to buy more equipment. I have found the key to success in the lawn care business is similar to any other industry. You have to aggressively market your business and strive to do the best job possible.

As far as marketing, I do it all. I use lawn signs in locations that I want to drum up more work. I run newspaper ads in the local paper. I visit all real estate companies. I also drive around town and look for more customers. I stop at apartments, doctors offices, truck stops etc… I will stop and ask for business wherever I can. I hand out cards to everyone I meet and give cards to all my friends and family to hand out.

I have found it to be very important to market to my existing customer base. This type of marketing is different because they know you and trust you. Marketing additional services to your existing customers can really improve your bottom line. For example I offer weeding of the flower beds, trimming low hanging trees, pressure washing, and gutter cleaning. I even cleaned a backyard pond and painted shutters. These are all services that I look for when I am on a job.

I always go the extra mile to help my customers and make their yards the best in the neighborhood. This helps me to go to them and ask them to help me find more work. They recommend me every chance they can. I ask them to refer me to their friends, family, employers, even if they do not have a lawn service at this time. I find that if they can get me in contact to offer a free quote I can work my magic and find more work. Once the door is open I have the opportunity to sell.

Most people would love to have someone cut their grass but think it is to expensive. I show them that it is not too expensive and that their yard can look a lot better. For every new contract that I sign from a customer's referral, I give them a $25.00 Visa card. I also advertise that I take Visa and Mastercard. This is a very good selling point for a lot of customers.

Much of my new business comes from the phone book and newspaper ads. This is also the most costly form of advertizing that I do. One or two annual lawn care contracts pays this for the entire year.

In addition to all that, I became a member of a national website's contractor group. They do the advertising and when a job comes up in my area they send me the contact information. I in turn pay them between $5 and $18 dollars for the contact if I land the job. This has worked out extremely well. I have not changed my cost at all when using this service. I bid against other locally approved companies. I don't get every one of the jobs, but with the cost of the leads being so low, I can quickly make up those costs. One annual contract more than pays for the full years worth of leads that I get from them.

I am not shy about my business. I tell everyone about it and I ask for the work. This is a big key to success."

Lawn care business quote cards.

If you have been looking for some ideas to create your own lawn care quote card, check out what this Gopher Lawn Care Business Forum member put together and was using to promote his spring lawn care services.

He wrote "my lawn care marketing plan this year is to visit a few neighborhoods and just write the mowing price on a lawn care quote card and leave it at the door. I am not looking to be the most expensive top notch lawn care operator out there. Instead I'd rather offer an affordable solution to homeowners in my area that don't have the time or means to care for their own lawns or just need some additional help.

I think by doing this with the quote cards, it may actually show customers that professional lawn care isn't expensive.

I usually try distributing the lawn care quote cards during the day sometime between 10 am and 4 pm. I haven't done any weekends yet.

I stopped at a Realtor's office earlier this week and talked to a few of the ladies in the office. We discussed a few ideas on how we could possibly work together to improve their home sales by improving the properties that surround the homes. They were very interested in boosting the curb appeal on their properties. They are finding it difficult now to sell homes and thought the idea of adding a year's worth of lawn and yard maintenance to help sweeten the home sale deal was a great idea. They felt it added a lot of value to the property at little additional cost to the seller. As I was leaving they asked for a quote for everything. Cutting, edging, trimming and some landscape work for a rock bed they have around their office building.

I've also talked to a few friends in different businesses and just general friends and family as I was passing by the place and they have said my quotes are very competitive for my area, so that helped me feel like I was on target.

The problem I am having though is I am not getting any calls. It's very confusing. I feel like I am missing something. The only thing I can come up with as to why is because I live on a state border town and I market in the other state at times. Do you think having an out of state area code on my cards could effect calls?"

I think that could play a big role in the success of your lawn care marketing campaign. If your phone number on the card shows an out of state area code, it might cost the home owner more money to call you and they also might feel you are too far away to provide the kind of service they need.

A number of factors may effect the success of your lawn care marketing campaign. Are you handing out enough cards? Quite often we see a response rate of between 1 - 2 %, so if you hand out 100 cards, you might get 1 or two return calls.

The time you are distributing the cards might be wrong too! The more you talk to people, the better your chances are of selling them your services. Look at the example you gave us with stopping in at the Realtor's office. You talked to them for a few minutes and they asked for a bid. That's the way to do it! Knowing this, you might decide to distribute your cards after dinner or on the weekends when the homeowner is available.

Lastly, if there is even a consideration that your phone number may be turning customers away, you need to change it. Get another cell phone or get one of those internet phone services that forward a number to your current cell phone.

Remove as many obstacles as possible between you and your

customers and you will find more success.

How important are signs on your lawn care truck and trailer?

How important is it to have signs and marketing material on your landscaping truck and trailer? This is a very good question that was asked on the Gopher Lawn Care Business Forum. A member wrote "things are really taking off here this Spring and it has been crazy in a good way. My question is has anyone used vinyl lettering on there trucks and or trailers? How does it hold up over the long haul? I'm looking to have this done to my truck as well as having some lawn signs made up, just waiting on the estimate to come back.

I thought about magnets, but I see them on the side of the road here and there. How cost effective is it?"

Another lawn care business owner responded by saying "All of our vehicles and trailers have vinyl signs on them. On the windows we also utilize one way signs so when you look out through from inside the trucks you would never know it's there.

It holds up great with no problems at all, even through car washes.

I have had a few customers tell me if they see magnetic signs on a vehicle they don't hire them because they feel the company is not serious about being in business and may not be in business long. Seeing vinyl lettering on a truck to them means a real company with commitment to success. That should give you something to think about.

I have found in business, image means a lot to both current and potential clients. We get a lot of comments on our trailers and trucks, especially on our logo. It was designed in part to attract kids due to the use of colors, which generally brings the parents, which leads to a conversation and perhaps a sales opportunity.

It's the same with the shirts and pants. I have the staff wear a nice uniform at all times and no sneakers on job sites. My staff never complain and I think they are proud to look professional as I receive feedback from them on customer comments quite often.

You need to remember that you are a walking and driving billboard for your company at all times. I have even picked up jobs from people who saw my truck at the post office of all places. I learned a lot of these marketing tactics from an employee I hired at another company I previously owned. He is simply amazing and never stops thinking about how to market our lawn care company."

So keep all these thoughts in mind when you are looking at your lawn care truck. All of your equipment is a blank slate screaming out to you to add signage to it. Signs on your vehicle and trailer promote a message of what you do and how to get into contact with you. Vinyl signs are more permanent than magnetic signs and tell the customer you plan on being in business for the long haul. Make it as easy as possible to let the customer know this vital contact information and use signs!

Marketing your lawn care business with only business cards?

During the most recent economic slump we see daily posts on the Gopher Lawn Care Business Forum about the difficulties lawn care business owners are having, trying to find new lawn care customers. One of our members had an opposing marketing view that is held by many and he is finding a lot of success now. Let's see how he is doing it.

He wrote "well these last few weeks I have been completely covered up with work. I have picked up several new commercial lawn accounts, plus 6 tree removal jobs at about $700 each (average). I have picked up 3 brush clearing jobs. One at $600, one at $1,900, and another at $4,250.

Most of my work comes from repeat business and referrals. Most of my new business comes from craigslist. I have never spent any money on advertising, except business cards. I have a theory that once you start paying for advertising, you will need to keep paying to keep the work flow coming, so I've tried to avoid it from day one.

I would suggest just putting yourself out there, and never turn down an opportunity to talk about work with someone. I have started up conversations with MANY people about what I do, and the next thing I knew I was giving a bid to them, or someone they knew.

So I guess, talk, talk, talk, and put yourself out there. Let everyone know what you are doing, and don't be afraid to ask someone if they need something done. A lot of the same things you have been saying on the forum."

What a fascinating insight! Now I would think not spending any money on advertising except for lawn care business cards would put him at a disadvantage, but it seems the opposite has happened. It is quite possible, to make up for the lack of customers he would have gotten by paying for advertising, he has had to compensate for it by being personable and working on his social networking skills. So I think this is a great lesson for us all. If you want to succeed and sell more, you need to talk more. Talk to anyone and everyone and let them know you can help solve their problems with your services.

How to use postcards effectively in your lawn care marketing.

One lawn care business owner shared with us his insight on how best to utilize postcards in your lawn care business marketing. He not only runs a lawn care business, he also runs a marketing business for lawn care business owners and has learned from years of experience doing this.

He wrote "the other day I had a customer ask if postcards are actually effective. I explained to him how they are actually one of the most efficient ways to get customers. I personally get 90% of my new 'lawn care' customers from direct mail/postcard mailings.

The one thing that people fail to do when using postcards is this… Don't send them to a potential customer only once!! It is IMPORTANT to mail them to the same list numerous times during the year. If you have a list of 600 names and addresses, split it up into 3 groups and send 200 per month and alternate it. This helps build name recognition, and the most importantly it helps you build denser routes.

The best part about this is the cost. If you only get 12 new customers a year, you still had a HUGE return on you investment.

Here is an example of how it breaks down for me:

5,000 postcards cost about $375 (design fee and printing)

If you mailed out 200 per month, the cards would last 2 years. Each month depending on postage costs would cost around $52 postage and $16 for the cards, TOTAL PER MONTH $68

I dare anyone to find a cheaper 'cost per sale!' (I know there are cheaper ways but you probably won't find one that is as effective.)

This brings me to my next point…DOOR HANGERS. Not that I think they are ineffective, because they can be very effective. But I do not think it's a less expensive route, like most do.

Let's assume your time is worth $10.00 per hour. Could you distribute 200 door hangers in 5.2 hours? ($52 postage divided by $10 per hour). I don't think so.

So this is my 2 cents. Take it for what it's worth. Utilize postcards in your marketing as I described and compare it to any other marketing method you have used to date. I bet you find it to be a pleasant surprise when you see the results."

A second lawn care business owner said "great points all around. Most small businesses make the mistake of doing 'one shot mailings.' It's a HUGE mistake.

Plus, they waste a ton of money trying to build a relationship with 5K prospects simultaneously instead of focusing on a smaller group (1,500 or so) over an extended period of time.

Run the numbers and you'll always come out ahead by spending more time with a smaller group. Become the big fish to a smaller pond, slowly expand the size of the pond, and soon enough you'll be the big fish in the big pond."

Tips on how to market to commercial lawn care clients.

Getting your foot in the door is an important step when you are marketing to commercial clients but how should you go about doing this?

One lawn care business owner asked "I need some help on getting more commercial lawn care accounts. I have one right now, only because one of my customers happened to also own a storage business. How do I get my name out to others though when everywhere you look it says no solicitations at every front door?"

A second lawn care business owner shared "with commercial accounts they really only care about two things: being reliable and cost of service.

I would first send them a letter, or brochure in the mail. Then I would follow up with a phone call approx 1 week later, asking them whether they received the letter and if they had any questions. Do not force yourself on them. Just explain your position, let them know that you are in the area and would love to offer them a FREE estimate, no strings attached. What would it hurt for them to get another price to compare to their current company?

Whatever you do though, do not bash their current lawn care company that is servicing the property. There are two reasons not to bash the other company:
  1) it will make you look bad.
  2) the person running the other company may be related to the owner or employees of the company you are soliciting to and this could cause a problem. Just be patient with them and discuss the issues you see with the state of their

property and what you would do to improve it.

I have a quick story on how I learned this lesson. One day after gassing up the truck and leaving the gas station I saw another landscaping that was having problems with his truck. It's not a big company they have about 15 accounts. We both were working on his truck but to no avail as we couldn't get it started. So he told me that he would pay me to do his lawns for the day.. AND PAID CASH. I happened to have that Saturday free so I bumped my Friday list to Sat and made some extra money. This wouldn't have happened if I had gone around town bad mouthing his business. We are all out there so if you see a landscaper needing help…. help him, you never know when that might happen to you.

After this all happened, I thought about how lucky it was for me that I never bashed my competition. Staying professional and being kind to others allowed me to earn a couple hundred extra bucks on a day I had free."

Advice on generating word of mouth advertising.

A lot of start up businesses really have a hard time generating word of mouth advertising. To help us understand how to do this better, I asked a member of the Gopher Lawn Care Business Forum how he did it.

I asked him, did you find it tough to generate word of mouth initially when you got started? What do you think is the best way to generate word of mouth advertising?

He responded by saying "I am originally from Southern Europe. I moved to the U.S. when I was 17 yrs old, now I am 28. I hold two college degrees and I love working with people. After I graduated from college, I told myself, I wanted to make money on my own. America is the place to do it.

That is why I started a landscaping business. I also have two rental properties, and working on buying a third one. I payed cash for my education. Despite the fact that I had to pay out of state tuition fees.

I had to earn my reputation in the town where I live. For a while, I had worked at a very famous restaurant, where I met and created a lot of contacts. When I was out around town and would run into my old restaurant customers, I would tell them what I was doing, and gave them my landscaping business cards. I always keep business cards in my wallet and my SUV. This led me to gaining a bunch of residential as well as commercial customers.

Then with the current customers I have, I make sure they are extremely pleased. This is important whether they are residential or commercial. I have one lady, she has two sons in Iraq, and lives on her Social Security income. It is very limited. She called me after I posted an ad in our local newspaper, and told me how much the other guy was charging her. I asked her how much she could afford to pay. She told me $40 per cut. It takes me 1 hour and a half to do that job. I told her I would do it. The last time I didn't hear from her for about almost a month. I called her up, and asked her, if she wasn't pleased with my work, or went with someone else. She told me she couldn't afford to pay me any longer. So I told her I can mow your lawn for free one time a month. She was so happy that she referred me to some of her friends, and I got 3 big jobs from her. For her birthday, I bought her one of her favorite liquor drinks she really likes.

Sometimes it isn't always about money, its about being kind, generous, and knowing who can pay and who can not pay, for what reasons? You know, in the end we are humans, and need to respect that. Yes we are in business to make money, but need to know where to get it from.

I love dealing with people, and it makes my day to see them smile and feel satisfied. I tell my guys that I hire part time, if my customers aren't happy and they complain about you, then you might as well hit the road.

In order to generate positive word of mouth business, here are a few more tips:

Be yourself.

Be professional.

The few customers you have, keep them satisfied. Despite, the fact that on some jobs you might have underbid, or are not making as much as you would like to. Do a great job. Don't just think about the money. If you do a great job, as they say 'hard work or quality work will speak for itself.'

Be friendly. When you pull up to give an estimate, don't pull up in a beat up truck, or trashy car. Look as professional as you much as you can.

Be understanding. Look at your customers. See what they wear, what they drive, where they live? Sometimes you can tell if they can pay or not based on what they drive, where they live, etc. I do this when I rent my apartments. I can tell who is going to be able to pay me the rent or not based on what they drive, how they dress, and what they do for a living.

When you run in to people at a store, or somewhere in town, be nice, be kind, help them if they need help, open the door for them, etc. Once you do that, then you can see if they want to talk to you or not. If so give them your business cards, make some shirts and always wear them with your business logo on it, and the phone number on it."

Common commercial lawn care marketing mistakes.

There are plenty of ways to market to commercial lawn care properties but many of them are a waste of time. Time is money and when you are spending time & money marketing, you want to make sure you are getting the greatest return for your efforts. Here is a great example from the Gopher Lawn Care Business Forum on how not to do things followed by suggestions on how to improve.

One lawn care business wrote us about his troubles landing new commercial lawn care accounts and said "I just got home from handing out my lawn care business cards and I feel like it was a total waste of time & cards.

Here is what I did and maybe someone can help me figure out what I am doing wrong. I walked into a few strip malls and plazas & asked to speak to the owner. Then I told the owner to have their land lord contact me as I handed them a business card.

After all that time and energy spent trying to make connections I only got a single call back. It was from the owner of a local commercial complex. Over the phone I agreed to a meeting with him. After that, I discontinued my efforts marketing to other buildings in the area and immediately went to that complex.

As I sat down for this meeting, the first thing this idiot tells me is, 'just to be fair, a contract is already signed for this year....' As soon as I heard that, I immediately left my card & stormed back home. What is the point of him wasting my time if he isn't going to hire me?

This process just doesn't feel right to me. Any suggestions on how to go about getting commercial lawn care accounts? Who should I be talking to? How should I get into contact with them?

Once I figure this out I would rather mow commercial properties than residential ones. I figure that is where the money is."

Another lawn care business owner responded and said "right off the bat, there are a couple of things I would like to point out about your marketing efforts. First off, you can't expect to hand out business cards the way you did and get the landlords to call you back. The fact that you got 1 return call is amazing actually.

You would improve your results quite a bit if you found the property owner yourself and marketed to them directly. Secondly, when you get a chance to meet with a property owner, don't be so quick to cut and run from the meeting. Listen to what he has to say. Pick his brain. Find out what he likes and dislikes about the lawn care maintenance he is currently getting and then present your own bid for the property. Point out how you will improve on what he wants and take care of the issues he dislikes about his current maintenance. Ask him if he has any other properties he needs a bid on or if he knows any other property owners in the area he could refer you to. There is gold in these meetings that is there for you if you are willing to mine it by asking the right questions.

When I first got started marketing to commercial lawn care customers, I found that I couldn't even get a response from any commercial property owners until I started carrying my certificate of insurance with me. Once I got that, I was at least able to take the next step to giving a presentation of my lawn care bid.

After you get your first commercial account, it's important to use it as a stepping stone to get more. My first commercial lawn care account was a small medical professional complex. The job included mowing, weeding and pruning a small lawn which was about 12′ deep around the building weekly and consisted of a total of 3,000 sq ft. I made sure to make the lawn look fantastic and got pictures of it for my marketing material and website.

The property size was perfect for me because it was inline with what I was used to mowing for my residential customers. My bid price was very accurate as far as price and length of time I thought it would take. I didn't feel like I was jumping into a property that was beyond my scope of competency. If the property were any larger, I easily could have underbid it and ultimately lost money on the job.

Now, when I want to market to larger commercial properties in my area, I use my county property appraiser's web site and it will tell me who owns the building or property. Once I look it up I can then research how I can contact the owner.

When you are first getting started though, you may find more success by sticking with mom and pop single free standing buildings. They usually have some grass to cut, trees to prune and maybe mulching along with flowers. They are smaller in size but easy to do and manageable. You will most likely bid them and profit comparably with your residential lawn care accounts. Later as you grow, you can always scale the size up."

BID EXAMPLES

Need help with first commercial lawn care bid.

Jumping from offering residential lawn care to commercial can seem to be a daunting task at first but nothing helps more than seeing and learning from the examples of others. Here is a great commercial lawn care bid example from a member of the Gopher Lawn Care Business Forum.

He wrote us about the job "this is my first commercial lawn care bid and I need help. There really isn't that much to mow, but a lot to trim. They would like trimming, mowing, blowing, as needed. Broadleaf weed control, fertilization 3x per year, collection and disposal of small debris, leaf removal in the fall, trimming/pruning of bushes.

How would you charge for a whole season that would include 28 mowings for each of the following? I have no idea on how much time each job will take but here is my best guess estimate of it. Does this price look possible? Total property size is 6.6 acres

  Mowing: 30-40 min = $1,600
  Trimming: 20 min
  Edging: 10 - 20 min = $840.00 (includes trimming)
  Small debris collection/disposal: 10 min = $280.00
  Weed Control: 30 min = $1,500
  Fertilization: 30 min = $2,000
  Leaf Removal: 45 - 60 min = $1,400
  Shrub Care: 20-30 min = $1,000

Total Contract Price = $8620.00
12 Monthly Payments = $718.00"

A second lawn care business owner suggested "I would estimate that job the same way you did by breaking each service down. Add up the time of each service and multiply it by your hourly rate.

I can't comment on the prices of your bid because I can't see the property and I don't know your hourly rate.

My advice would be to bid this job the same way you would bid a residential. A lot of guys who are new to commercial lawn care think that they should charge more for a commercial mowing job than residential. If you do that, you won't get or keep too many commercials lawn care accounts with that business strategy. You need to know your costs. Don't low ball your services and you'll be fine. As time goes on you will get a better feel for the time it takes to do jobs.

Also, use the lawn care business calculators available here on the Gopher Forum to help you refine your bidding process."

Apartment complex bid example.

Jumping from residential lawn care to offering commercial lawn care can be tough on a newer lawn care business owner because you just aren't used to estimating larger properties. With no example to go by, you may greatly underestimate the amount of time it would take to mow and the amount you should charge.

In a discussion on the Gopher Lawn Care Business Forum a member posted an overhead image of an apartment complex he was wanting to bid on but since he had no previous commercial lawn care bidding experience he needed help.

He wrote "can you help give me an example quote for this property. I need to include mowing, weeding, edging, and blowing. This apartment complex is a 6 unit complex with a pool and an entrance way. There are two major hills on the corners, one far left and one far right."

A second lawn care business owner responded "before I give you the example let me share with you some concerns. First never give an estimate based strictly on an overhead photograph. It can give you a general idea of what you are bidding on but you have to visit the site yourself to understand the lay of the land, obstructions, gradients, type of grass, desires of the apartment management, etc.

Secondly, I can't see the slope of the hills you describe. Also, there looks to be a drainage problem in the upper left corner of the complex. Problems like these can add hours to your work and you simply cannot plan for them based on a photo.

One other thing, there are aspects I can't take into account due to it being only a photo such as:

Weeding - I can't even see the beds. So, I'm going to leave them off.

Travel Time - Umm...no way for me to determine this either.

For this example, I am assuming 1 person running a 61″ lawn mower with a 20hp motor, 1 weed eater, and 1 backpack blower. The equipment operator is proficient and mows with a 80% efficiency. What I mean by this is you need to take into consideration overlaps, inefficient turns, etc. when calculating mowing time. I am also going to assume this area is 40% more difficult to mow than a 'normal' area this size.

Okay, now that all that is out of the way, I crunched some numbers based on your photo. Here is what I have come up with:

1) Mowing: I calculated the size of the entire project is approximately 16 acres (outlying trees not included). Taking out buildings, parking lots, sidewalks, etc, the actual mowing area is almost 11.5 acres. I believe you can mow that area in an estimated 5 1/2 hours taking into account for the difficult terrain and the equipment described above.

2) Trimming/Edging: My calculations for trimming accounted for buildings, walk paths, pool and other public areas but it did not account for the outside perimeter or the perimeter at the outside of the parking lot. Taking this into account, I came up with 6,220 feet of string trimming that needs to be done every week. Trimming at the speed of 1′ per second, the total trimming time will take about 1 hour 43 minutes.

3) Blowing: Blowing is subjective. By minimizing the amount of grass your mower shoots onto walk areas, you should be able to blow off the area in 1 hour. Size of blower and number of cars in the way will have a bearing.

Alright, let's add all this up:

Mowing: 5.5 hours
Trimming: 1.72 hours
Blowing: 1.00 hours
Total: 8.22 HOURS

Based strictly on one photograph you sent and some assumptions,
I came up with an estimated 8 hours 13 minutes to do this job.
Now all you need to do is multiply that time by your cost per hour
to operate and you will get your final price."

A look at a $72,200 commercial lawn care contract.

Whether you are just looking to get into offering commercial lawn care or you are currently offering it and wanting to see what others are charging for their services, here is a great inside look at one condominium associations commercial lawn care contract. In this example discussed at the Gopher Lawn Care Business Forum, a condo association agreed to a $72,000 a year lawn care contract.

This condo association consists of 82 condos. The lawn care contractor is to be paid in ten installments, with a $7,220 invoice sent monthly from March through December.

The lawn care services to be provided in this lawn care contract consist of the following:

$16,340 - Turf Mowing
$3,760 - Early spring cleanup
$23,904 - Mulching
$2,066 - Lawn edging
$5,152 - Weeding of mulch beds
$1,055 - Pruning in early Summer
$355 - Pruning in mid Summer
$355 - Pruning in late Summer
$1,055 - Pruning in late Fall
$1,235 - Fall lawn aeration
$1,450 - Fertilization - Spring
$1,450 - Fertilization – Summer #1
$4,200 - Fertilization – Summer #2
$1,450 - Fertilization - Fall
$952 - Fall leaf pickup #1
$952 - Fall leaf pickup #2
$952 - Fall leaf pickup #3

$952 - Fall leaf pickup #4

$67,635 - Total year contract not including taxes.

Also to be provided are winter snow plowing services at the additional rate of:

$80 - Plow salt truck per hour
$0.12 - Salt per pound
$35.00 - Hand Shovel Labor per hour
$0.45 - Ice melt per pound

Commercial lawn care bid example of an ocean resort.

We all tend to learn best by example so here is a commercial lawn care bid example that was posted on the Gopher Lawn Care Business Forum. If you haven't gotten into creating lawn care bids for commercial properties, this will at least shed some light on the process.

A member wrote "I tried searching the forums to see if a situation like mine has occurred here but I didn't find one so maybe someone has an idea of what I can do.

The scenario is this. I was working as a groundskeeper of a condominium association with a monthly base pay of $550. This included cutting, edging, trimming and pruning. It takes me a bit of time to cut due to the layout of the property but not a major issue.

At the beginning of the month the property manager informs me that the property owner's association is sending out the grounds keeping to bid and he gave me the list of what would be required.

Here is what they want included in the property maintenance bid.

Subcontractor Grounds Maintenance Duties

- Mow and trim all common grounds areas including the backyards of town homes.
- Pickup and cleanup (vacuum not blow) all common area grounds (including walkways, town home backyards, swimming pool areas, etc.) four times per week during May through August and 2 to 3 times per week during the rest of the year.

- Empty wastebaskets at swimming pools and mail area.
- Weed or use herbicide as needed in all areas.
- Trim bushes and plants as needed. (Does not include the Palms but does include the Sagos)
- Check and test irrigation once per week—advise maintenance of any problems.
- Report any needed repairs in a written list.
- All equipment, gasoline and chemicals provided by subcontractor.
- Successful bidder must provide copy of liability insurance before commencement of work begins.

All bids must be submitted by March in a sealed envelope to the Homeowners Association either in person to the office or by mail. The bid will be awarded beginning of April for a one year period with renewals for one year periods possible with consent of both parties.

My question is really how much should I charge on this. If I got the contract I would have to use my equipment and furnish all materials. So I am assuming a definite price increase.

As far as time I would need to spend on a mowing day it takes me about three hours which is cutting, trimming, edging, and blowing of the drives. This is really because of the layout of the town home section which has 18 individual turf islands.

On a non-cut day it takes me about two to three hours to complete my tasks. I tend to time those tasks out over the course of the week as the association required me to be there for the specified days. So regardless of whether or not I had zero work to be done, if I didn't show up, the property manger was calling me because the owners were on his case.

The way that the list for bidding is written, the contractor would be required to be there for four days per week during the summer and two to three times during the rest of the year. So the way I worked this was I essentially had to find things to do because I did not want to drive 15 miles one way for 15 to 30 minutes of work. On the other hand there are some days that I may work 8 hours or more. So if I were able to show up and fulfill the tasks at hand and not return until the next cutting cycle, I would venture to say maybe 2 to three hours per week. Once again that is just if I did it like it should be done. However as I stated, the property manager wants to see you because the owners nag if they don't see me.

I also must add that during the winter months down here the beaches are generally quiet so I show up twice a week to do some cleaning up and viola I'm out in about an hour.

I figured it up at around 172 hours per year to do this job. That would be just going out and doing the job and leaving and not showing up just to show up."

Well if you plan on 172. That is (172/12 months) = 14.3 hrs per month.

Say you times that by an average lawn care rate per hour of about $45.

(14.3 x $45) = $645 per month.

What do you think of billing them something like that?

"That is right around what my wife was talking and that makes a lot of sense. I appreciate and hopefully I will get the contract."

BIDDING ADVICE

When to bid on commercial lawn care contracts?

When you are running a lawn care business in one geographic area and more to another, you may find the mowing season can differ greatly from what you were used to. That is what one lawn care business owner found when he mentioned on the Gopher Lawn Care Business Forum, how he was moving from the northeast to a more southern state. He was interested in knowing when he should time his move to get a jump start on the next years commercial lawn care contracts.

He wrote "I have a lawn care business in the New England area that I am selling. This area has a lot of money and there always seems to be plenty of work to go around. However there are a good number of people here that run a lawn service business and more appearing every day. I am planning on moving to a more southern state to start a new lawn care business. That area is very economically diverse. It ranges widely from the very wealthy, who have someone come in to mow their lawns and everything else. To people who are just scraping by and don't even have enough to buy the materials for a do-it-yourself project.

There are of course a lot of in-betweeners, middle class, as well. This group is similar to the people that I currently serve. I have flexibility as to when I make my move. When I move, I want to put in lawn care bids on commercial properties. I have never put bids on commercial properties up in the northeast before because I didn't want to offer snow plowing.

So my question is, when do commercial accounts typically take bids in the southern area?

Another lawn care business owner wrote "the weather in a lot of the southern states allows for grass cutting to taper off in November but can continue into December and start up again by early March. I've even seen warm winters when I've been cutting wild garlic sprouts in customer's yards in mid-January.

Our winters lend to erratic mowing contract schedules. Quite honestly, contract bid acceptances are all over the calendar down here. Many contracts are let out for bid in January with March 1 as the first mowing date. While other contracts are March through October with free-lance work done the other 4 months. Bids are accepted into February.

The U.S. government's fiscal year begins October 1. So, government agency contracts are often let out for bid in August or September.

If you are timing your move, I would advise moving sooner rather than later. December is generally slow but it's a good time to get your name in front of the people who will be making the buying decisions in a month or two."

How I found commercial lawn care property bids in my area.

Finding commercial lawn care bids is not as difficult as you may think. Most times it comes down to picking up the phone and finding who to talk to or simply visiting the establishment and asking a few questions. That is what a member of the Gopher Lawn Care Business Forum did when he found a fast food business who needed a lawn care bid for five of their properties.

He wrote "I am going to be bidding on 5 locations for a fast food chain. The work to be done is mowing, trimming and blowing off the parking lot and walkways of grass clippings, once per week. Each site is between 1.3 - 1.6 acres. I am estimating that each site will have about 30 min. of mowing.

To find this job, what I did was call up the restaurant, introduced myself, first name, and name of my business. Then I told them that I would like to put a bid in for their lawn care this season and asked who I could speak with about that. They gave me the name and number of their franchise owner and I gave him a call and left a similar message.

He called back that same day and said that he would be interested in getting quotes. An added bonus for me is that he said he owned four other locations and said he would like bids on those also.

Being new to commercial lawn care, this is how I have came to have the chance to submit all of my quotes. I literally drove around the areas that I was interested in. I wrote down information about the locations. When I got home later, I looked them up in the phone book or got the number off their signs. After that I started making calls. By doing that, I am now bidding on a church (6-7 acres), those 5 fast food locations, another fast food location, and a small hotel. I was nervous at first, but everyone has been very polite. If they do their own lawn care, I thank them for their time, leave my card and let them know if they are ever interested to please feel free to call.

For the fast food jobs, I figure it would take about 30 minutes of mowing for each site. Trimming, I am estimating about 10-15 minutes (most of the trees are mulched around). I think that by myself I could be in and out of there in about an hour. My payment terms are within 15 days of the invoice, billed the first of each month. I plan to stop mowing if payments are not received though. I learned a tough collection lesson last year and am still trying to collect $400 from a previous customer.

I measured the mulch beds and am quoting that they would need another 1″-2″ of mulch installed. I calculated the amount of mulch needed by figuring the total sq. ft. of each bed and dividing that by 165 to get how many yards I would need. Then I calculated how much to charge for this by doubling the price I pay for mulch to cover the time spent laying it.

As far as bush trimming I quote them per bush. Example: bushes knee high or less = $3.00 per bush. Knee to waist high = $5.00 per bush. Waist and higher = $10-$20 per bush. I am going with that method until I can get a better idea of how long it takes me to trim them.

So, all in all I will bid a price for mowing, trimming and blowing, then a price for bush trimming (each occurrence) and another price for mulch. I did not ask about the trash removal from the parking lot, but I will see if they are interested in that service too. I would pick up any trash if it were on the lawns. But I can already tell there will probably be a high occurrence of this so I need to account for the time to perform this in the bid as well."

Another lawn care business owner suggested "your bid should

include: mulching twice a year, bush trimming once a month, weeding twice a month, leaf pick up twice in the fall and litter clean-up every week. Make it a package deal, find out how much it would cost them for a full year and divide it by twelve and put them on a twelve month paying schedule so you get payed every month for a full year. Make sure you continue to do stuff like leaf clean up, litter pick up and stuff like that even through the winter months."

Who should you present your commercial lawn care bid to?

This is a great discussion about who should you present your commercial lawn care bid to. Knowing who to present your bid to can make all the difference in the world. The right person can give you the job on the spot. The wrong person can throw your bid out the moment you walk out their door.

One lawn care business owner wondered "should you have a bid ready when you are going out prospecting? How do you know what services they want or don't want?

For example there is a store next to where I live and I know the owner. Just from going in there frequently and buying stuff. I want to talk to him to see if he would like me to bid on his property.

So should I be walking in with a bid already made out with optional services already listed, etc. or no?

There are a bunch of concerns I have about this. What if I bid the hedges to be cut 4 times a year and he only wants them done twice a year?

Also where do I include information about my company? Or is this not necessary?

Maybe it would be better to use a brochure instead?

If I go down there and talk to someone on a cold call in person, what kind of package or info do you think I should be leaving whoever I spoke with."

A second lawn care business owner shared "I am glad you asked this question.

First off, never leave your bid with anyone other than your contact. Always, even on a cold call, ask to speak with the person that can make the decision. Once you get them, ask any and all questions you may have.

As far as this store, you already have a rapport with this person so you can be a little more informal but still present yourself in the manor I know you will and that is 100% professional.

If this were me, I would create a quote letter. It is brief and to the point, no mumbo jumbo. Then I also would attach an estimate work sheet along with it.

Remember: you're only giving an estimate on what services YOU feel should be provided to give 'CURB APPEAL.' You can always negotiate the number of times the service will occur. For example if you estimate hedge trimming 4 times a year and they only want it twice, in the spring and fall, then you can cut your price by half on that service. Only bid or show an estimate for each service to be provided.

DO NOT show the monthly price.

You can give a monthly price after they agree on what services and the # of times each service is to be preformed. You can break it down to 8 or 12 equal payments. You can also make notes, if needed, on the estimate sheet and then make the adjustment when you write up the contract in the SCOPE OF WORK section.

BTW tuck in a complete contract already prepared just as if they were to accept the estimate in full. This way if they agree to every thing, you can leave there in one trip with a signed contract, DEPOSIT CHECK, and signed estimate approval in hand. DONE

DEAL.

NOTE: If it were me and since you know him, I would create and estimate through Gopher Lawn Care Software. Itemize each service and frequencies of each service, attach it to a quote letter, with a cover binder and hand it to him directly. Include 3 business cards and start negotiations right then and there at the end of the conversation. If he/she seems stuck on the edge one way or the other DON'T FORGET TO ASK FOR THE SALE a lot of times when there is a hang up this will close the deal.

You could also add a little something about your company in the last page of your bid package, sometimes visuals are sellers."

What % of the time do you think a deal could be made on the spot like that?

Should a lawn care operator ever consider more of a soft sell where they present it to them and let the business owner get back to them? Or is it more important to say, this is what I think your property needs and here is my price, and then see if they will sign a contract with you then and there?

He replied "50-50 for me. Hard sell or soft sell it's all in the feel for that customer. If you think you can get a contract then and there, go for it.

If you feel the customer will need time, then give them time and don't even mention a contract. Give them a few days, 4-5 and give them a return call if they haven't called you.

It is all in how comfortable you are and the customer is with you, whether you present a contract right then or you wait."

What should you include in a commercial lawn care bid?

When you are looking to submit a bid for a commercial lawn care property maintenance contract, here are some words of advice as to what to include and improve your chances of success.

One lawn care business owner wrote "a brochure is a nice added touch to the professionalism of your company presentation. I like to leave a little more than that though when visiting commercial accounts.

Not only do I leave a business card (that is a given) but I leave 3 cards. I put together a small portfolio, that almost looks like copies of my web pages. It includes all the services we can and will provide, never leave it up to the customer to assume anything. I build all this in a power point presentation file, highlighting key benefits of our services over and above the competition. I include only a couple of pictures of current clients and I also include a list of references.

A lot of times I see business owners make the mistake of listing 'references available upon request' in their bid. The way I look at it is if it were I who was accepting bids or meeting with different companies for a service provider, and I had to ask about references when I have a company that has already provided them to me, why would I request references from others if I have it in front of me? Whether they were low bidders or not they would have a better or best chance of winning my business. It saves me time and 'Shows Completion.' The portfolio also includes copies of my business licenses for the area and insurance certificates. Now I have a COMPLETE package for their review.

You will find most businesses have to do things on certain

standards, by this I mean before any work can begin, all the proper paperwork needs to be in order. If you go in there with your paperwork already in order, it is an advantage you will have over and above the others. Keeping you one step ahead of the competition is right where you want to be.

The more professional you appear, the larger your company will appear. With this paperwork and such a presentation, the prospective client will forget how small you are. If all paperwork is in order and they need you to start, they may send you a letter of intent prior to sending out the signed contract and this is good to go."

Here is a list of what I put into a commercial bid package.

Commercial lawn care bid packages should include:
1. Certificate of Insurance
2. Occupational License
3. Itemized list of work to be completed (Estimate)
4. Contract with detailed scope of work (include time schedules)
5. Additional or optional services (with pricing and time schedule)
6. Cover letter (thank you)

This may seem redundant but it is professional and clearly answers most questions a client may have, without them having to take the time to call you to define such questions.

Benefits of this presentation:
1. Most lawn care operations only submit a cover letter and a quote/estimate (This puts you over and above or one step ahead.)
2. It shows clear detail you're prepared, confident and ready to get started.
3. It cuts down on the 'down time' having to travel back and forth getting this doc or that doc to the client, wasting valuable time for both parties. TIME IS MONEY!

Ask yourself these 2 questions:

Who would I want to do business with, someone who scribbles a quick estimate down on the back of a business card or piece of notebook paper or someone who has taken the time to put together a professionally completed bid package with all required documents included?

I'll let my track record stand with the second choice. Which currently is at a 95% + success rate."

What is the best way to create a lawn care bid for an apartment or condo complex?

One lawn care business owner looking to start bidding on apartments wanted to know "what is the best way to create a lawn care bid for an apartment or condo complex?"

A second lawn care business owner suggested "This question is one that many have as they get ready to break out of the residential market and into commercial/condos.

As you might have guessed there is no easy answer or magic formula that will produce a bid on larger multi-dwelling properties. Experience is key, which is why getting a year or two under your belt doing residential mowings is advisable. After that, you should be very competent at bidding and doing residential jobs and the same principles will help you bid the bigger properties.

There are a couple of methods you can try as you bid on these properties. Both require breaking the job down into smaller, easy-to-handle portions.

The first is to estimate the time it takes to do each of the different jobs and then add up your time over the year. For example, if you think it will take 3 hours to cut and edge the lawn, then multiply this 3 hours by the number of times you expect to cut the lawn throughout the year. Add on the time it takes to do other tasks such as trimming, pruning, bed care, fertilizing, general clean-up, blowing off and so on. Don't forget anything! Create a worksheet you can use that lists all the jobs and figure out how long each will take.

Once you have your total time for the year, you can multiply it by your hourly rate. Don't forget to add on materials and equipment overhead as well. If your hourly rate does not include general overhead then you need to add this onto the total too. When you supply the quote to the customer, show the cost as an annual fee and have it broken down. For example, after listing all the services you intend to supply say: The cost for this year-round property maintenance program will be $4,685/year or $390.41/month over 12 months. (Or something like this)

Another method is to use formulas. This might require a little more experience because it is important that your formulas are accurate. Remember, your quote will only be as accurate as your formulas. However, if you are confident with your pricing you can create formulas like:

Cost per 1,000 square feet to cut lawn = ?
Cost per 1,000 square feet to fertilize lawn = ?
Cost per linear foot to trim a hedge = ?

You get the idea? You'll have to measure everything accurately but once you get some good formulas, the job gets pretty easy. Of course you may need to make adjustments (the cost to cut a heavy slope would be more than a flat lawn) so you will have to use your judgment.

You may find that using a combination of both methods works for you."

Should you give your mowing price per sq. ft. to a customer?

Lawn care customers come up with the craziest requests at times. This seems to happen more so when the economy is down. Then they want to come up with their own methods to find a way to lower their costs while increasing the amount of work you are putting into their property. As we will see from this discussion on the Gopher Lawn Care Business Forum, sometimes it's simply better to say no than to put yourself and your lawn care business in a bad spot.

One lawn care business owner wrote "so I was charging a company a flat rate of $65 per property for mowing, and $35 to trim, blow, weed around porches, beds for a couple of years now. Most of the properties that I service for this company have hedges all the way around the border that I need to line trim underneath. All of them have porches and ramps as well.

This year they want me to submit my bid with a per square foot price for mowing and a price with a linear ft charge per trimming and edging. One property is 20,195 sq ft and another is 33,000 sq ft. There is also a smaller one that is around 13,000 sq ft but it has a lot more trimming and edging needed.

I have no idea what the going rate is per square foot or linear foot in my area. Furthermore I have to drive 40 minutes to get to the job sites. I have no idea what to charge for linear foot for the trimming either! Why do they want me to do this? Is this normal?

I tried to explain that to the company, since we did snow removal for them at a flat rate, we had flat rated the larger /smaller lawns too. We mainly based this price on the amount of time it took to perform and charged by the hour. They informed me that this year their budget was cut by half, therefore they wanted to know why we charged them the same for one smaller property as we did for the other three larger ones. I told them I gave them a break and charged less for the larger properties while I charged a fair price for the smaller one. But now they think I should charge per square foot and linear foot. If I did it that way, I am sure it would cost them more, not less. So I don't know how to explain it any clearer that they are getting a break already.

I am starting to get a feeling there's a lowballer that is wanting in. I just don't know what to do."

Another lawn care business owner said "there isn't a way to just give a company a price per sq. ft. that covers all situations. Each property could be bid on and then broken down to show a price per linear foot and square foot but that wouldn't be giving them what they want.

What if one property has a flat lawn and the next one has a hill with a 25 degree slope in the backyard with 50 trees and then a drainage ditch that needs to be manually trimmed? The price at each property would vary per unit of measurement.

Knowing a price per square foot when all things are equal is one thing but there has to be a fudge factor allowance to be used when you deem it to be.

It sounds to me like someone in accounting is attempting to understand your mowing lawn estimation formula. They are probably doing this to either pigeonhole you into doing more work for less money or they are (like you said) probably shopping work out to lower priced competitors.

Either way, it is your prerogative to decline giving them your formula. Tell them you only give prices on a per property basis and let that be the end of it."

How to bid one customer with multiple properties.

At some point while you are operating your lawn care business, you are going to come across a customer who owns multiple properties and will want you to bid on all of them at once. These properties might be residential or they may be commercial. How should you present your bid to such a customer and look professional doing it even when you may be unsure how they want the bid presented? That is a question asked on the Gopher Lawn Care Business Forum.

A lawn care business owner shared with us his situation when he wrote "I am a fairly new business owner. This is my third year in business. I have a web site but do not advertise any where else. I have gotten plenty of business all through word of mouth. The secret to it is if you just go the extra mile with each and every customer, before you know it, people will just come out of the wood work looking for your business and pay very well for your services.

Recently I had a property manager call and ask if I would submit bids for all of their lawn accounts. This totals 38 accounts in all! I did not want to look unprofessional or anything, so I didn't ask how he wanted the bid presented. But now I am wondering how the bids should look. Should I list all the accounts on one page with a break down of service fees with a weekly and monthly price quote? Or should I have each bid separate from all others on separate paper?"

A second lawn care business owner suggested "first off, you shouldn't ever worry about asking the customer how they want the bids presented. This won't make you look like an amateur. The fact that they didn't tell you how they wanted it most likely means they have no idea themselves which way would work best. You always should ask the customer what they want and give it to them.

With the situation you are in now, you could print it out both ways so you are prepared either way the property manager wants it presented.

Usually the property manager will present you with a cover letter along with the bid package, detailing how to submit. However, if one is not available, as I said, it doesn't hurt to ask. In my experience you should provide a separate quote for each property. These properties may be held under different board of directors / owners and the property management company will have to present them to each."

Need help winning church and commercial lawn care bids?

There are many paths you can take your lawn care business when you want it to grow. You can focus on residential. Or maybe focus on commercial lawn care. Many newer lawn care business owners like to try and get their feet wet in commercial work as soon as they have a few residential customers. But how can you find them? Also how can you find mowing jobs for church properties? That is what one member of the Gopher Lawn Care Business Forum wanted to know.

He wrote "I am just starting my lawn care business and am working with a limited budget. I got the essential lawn care equipment and made a few business cards. I will start making flyers in a few days as well. I have been pretty amazed as it is going better than I expected so far. I need some help from here though. I know how to get residential accounts but I am now interested in getting churches and shopping malls (people that actually have the money to pay the bills) as clients. How do I go about contacting these places? What kind of paperwork do I need when biding or estimating for commercial properties?"

A second lawn care business owner said "personally, I have always found churches tough to get strictly for grass cutting. It seems that every church has a congregation member who will do their lawn maintenance at crazy reduced rates. One angle I have found that works is to offer landscaping to the mix. Property beautification (instead of just grass cutting) is appealing to many churches.

I have a good amount of experience bidding larger jobs like what you are targeting. At the beginning of the year if you really want to get the larger scale and more profitable contracts in your area, that is the time to get cracking and contact property management agencies. Get your name on their bidder's lists. Contact anyone you are seriously interested in having as a client and speak with their purchasing departments. This is normally your first action in getting your foot in the door."

Another business owner shared about his experience getting churches as customers. "I just put in a lawn care bid for a church for $700.00 a month. I will start the job in June once the current contract is up. It's a simple contract for total lawn care. Mowing, edging, weed eating and so on. This year I am focusing on commercial jobs. So far I have two shopping malls, one trucking company, and that church. From here on in I think I'm going to stay with commercial lawn care only.

To get the church job, I dealt with a single person. As for the bid, I had cut it in the past while working with another company but the last two times, the owner never payed me. So I went to the church myself and offered my services. I already knew who to contact and how much they were charging so it was a lot easier for me."

A fourth lawn care business owner shared his advice when it came to getting into commercial property maintenance. He wrote "start off small at first. This is very important to keep in mind. When I say small I mean look for smaller commercial sites initially. The fastest way to kill a business is to jump too fast into the large commercial property care end. There are a lot of expenses involved in this and the two biggies that come to mind are PAYROLL and PAYROLL TAXES.

You will also need the capital to carry you through a minimum of 60 days and this means not having any income for that period of time. It all comes straight out of your pocket. If you can't cover the employee's salaries while you wait for your invoices to be paid, you won't have anyone to do the jobs. Don't ever bank on what you think you will get in the mail, bank on what you have in hand. You never know what may happen between doing the work and getting paid for it.

Then there is the added equipment for the added crews, truck, trailer, Z's, trimmers, etc.. You can finance all this but you don't want to over exceed your income. When you finance and you're a younger lawn care business operation, you don't want bank loans for equipment. Instead you should be looking to lease the equipment and use the tax breaks that come along with leasing. You can write off 100% of your lease payments. If you buy, you can only write off a small % of that equipment per year.

Most smart lawn care business owners will lease equipment for 3 years, no more than that and buy it out after the lease is up. Keep it for 2-3 more years and then trade it in on a new lease and complete the cycle again. When adding equipment you can put money down on the lease and start a new cycle.

Now here is the kicker, if you lease for say 3 years do the 100% write off, buy it out when the lease is up. Keep it for 2 more years minimum before trading in, the depreciation value for tax purposes is a higher % than if you just paid cash or got a loan on it in the beginning.

Most lawn care business owners move equipment every 6-9 years based on the condition of the equipment, which brings up maintenance on equipment and how important it is. If your equipment is in poor condition then the trade in will be low and you will have to sit on it trying to sell it privately and you don't want that headache.

Starting off small by adding equipment as you go is the best way. This could take realistically 3-5 years to accomplish after you have established a good track record in the residential area. There are exceptions to this rule, but generally speaking this is just how it is."

Don't know what to charge that commercial property? Ask them.

This is a very novel approach to estimating a commercial lawn care job. I don't often see this happen but I guess it goes to show you, it never hurts to ask. This is especially true when you are talking to a new client that is switching lawn care service providers. If you take the time to ask them what they did or didn't like about their previous lawn care company, you can learn what you should or shouldn't be doing on site. If you are lucky, you might also be able to get a glimpse at how much they were previously paying for lawn care. That's what a member of the Gopher Lawn Care Business Forum did.

He wrote "I need help putting together a bid on my first apartment complex. The total sq ft. is 65,545 divided into sections from 1,000 sq ft to 3,500 sq ft. I think it will take 2 guys around 4 hours. I have an idea what I should be charging but I am afraid I might be underbidding and should charge more. Also they want their side walks edged and beds edged. They also want flowers planted by their office.

I wasn't sure what I should be charging so I asked the manger what their previous lawn care company was charging per cut and she told me $250.00 per cut. She said they were very unhappy with them. I am thinking I could underbid the previous business and go with $230.00 per cut. They should be happy with that price and they will will be very happy with my work."

In such a situation, you could have a bunch of things working against you. First off, in such a situation, the manager could easily be lowballing you on the price and giving you a figure to see if you will take it. You need to know your costs so when you figure out how much time the job will take, you can plug in your hourly operating costs to come up with a acceptable price for your business to charge.

If you do have a figure in your head to charge and the manager's figure is higher, why go lower? Why not offer the same price and then sell the manager on how much better your service will be?

But at the very least this discussion is great to point out the value of asking questions. Ask all the questions you need to come up with for a proper estimate. Find out what will make the manager happier with you and this may well turn out to be a happy business relationship.

How to land commercial lawn care accounts without a mower.

You might read this title and think to yourself, there is no way one can land a commercial lawn care account without having a mower, but this new lawn care business owner did just that. How did he do it? He knew the right people. But how did he meet the right people? That's the trick.

What he did can be replicated and you can do it too. This is a lesson in offering multiple services and making yourself available to your customers.

A new lawn care business owner wrote to us of his experience on the Gopher Lawn Care Business Forum and said "I have been doing snow plowing for 6 years now and one of my customers asked if I would mow his property this summer. It is a commercial property and I looked it over and asked a lot of questions because I had never offered this service before and he gave me a general idea of the amount of time it was taking the previous lawn care operation to mow the property. So from that information, I created a bid and went in to drop my bid off and BAMMM. The manager said let's do it and signed the lawn contract right then and there.

Now this was not for one property, it was for two commercial properties. Just like that I was $25K in the black and I had no mowers. So next up I was off to the local commercial mower store and haggled two zero turns, one with a 48″ deck and a last year model for a discount, both come with warranties, for a great price.

I got excited about offering more lawn care services and put an ad in the paper on Monday. A couple of days later I had a customer signed up and I just got my second call Saturday for lawn care as well. I will meet with him next week to get a signed contract. Can you believe this? One week of ads and already two more customers. I hope it keeps up, as the season gets warmer I am sure I will be getting more calls.

I am also working on door hangers and hope to get them printed this week. My logo is done and we are off to market mowing services for next season. I will be distributing my door hangers using the cloverleaf method of house distribution. (Where you place them on the doors, 3 houses to the left, 2 houses to the right, and 3 houses across the street from your current customer, after you finish mowing.) I am going to be offering spring and fall cleanups as well as gutter cleaning. I am pushing for 40 residential accounts this year and 80 next year. I am more aggressive than most guys around here with my marketing so I believe that is in my favor.

This all started with a question and ended with a signed deal in the first two weeks of winter, after a snow fall."

A lot of newer lawn care business owners have a tough time getting into commercial property maintenance. Can you give us your insights as to how they should go about doing this?

"If you are first trying to get into commercial property maintenance you really need to know someone. That always helps you get a job quickly. Commercial property managers tend to dislike their last lawn guy. If you can get in tight with them by offering one service, say for instance, snow plowing, and they like your snow plowing then it will open other doors.

When the property manager asked if I could handle their lawn care maintenance, the first question I asked was how long did it take the previous company to mow the property? The answer was two days.

I looked at this person and said how many people did you have working on it? They said 4 but they were hired help (meaning lazy). This property should take 4 hrs to trim it all. So we will have two people doing trimming while the other two run the mowers. When it is done, two will push mow certain small areas where the ZTR can't reach. The other two will blow off drives and sidewalks.

Most people around here are honest and will tell you prices and man hours. They want job their property maintained properly.

Ask the right questions in a non-threatening way and you will get most of your answers. If they refuse to disclose, then move on to another question, but always ask the question they didn't answer in another way after they feel more comfortable with you.

By doing this, I have not had anyone say no to any of my questions."

Always follow up after you submit a lawn care estimate.

Once you are contacted by a potential client and meet with them to bid on their property, you aren't done yet. Remember to always follow up. This applies to both commercial and residential lawn care customers.

One lawn care business owner asked "I was just wondering after someone calls you for a lawn care estimate and you go out to meet with them, and then submit a bid, do most of them let you know if you didn't get the job or do they just kinda blow you off?"

A second business owner answered "A few things can happen:

1. They will say something like 'Geez, that is higher than I thought it would be.' At this point you can either haggle with the price or tell them, 'sorry, that is the price,' and stick to your guns.
2. They will say something like 'when can you start.' They agree to the price and want you to do it.
3. Or they say 'I will have to talk it over with my husband/wife.' Nine times out of ten when someone says that, you probably will not get the bid. Now they may either call you back and tell you yes or no, or not bother calling at all.

I recommend that after a few days, give them a call up and ask them if they had any questions in regarding the bid. It helps get the ball rolling again."

"Okay how about commercial accounts? When they are excepting bids and say we're not deciding until the middle of March. Should

I call them back then or just hope to hear from them and if I didn't get it will they call and tell me. Or just let it go?"

In reply he said "if you haven't heard anything after a while, then I would follow up with a phone call and even perhaps a letter. Sometimes they want to see how interested you are and that just might make the deal for you.

Following up with clients is a great way to improve your chances of landing the lawn care bid. Use your call as an opportunity to go over any questions they might have or any sticking points and close the sale."

Why the cheapest lawn care bid doesn't always win.

New lawn care business owners tend to enter the market by bidding their jobs lower than others. This may work at times but as you grow, you will see problems with this lawn care business plan. The first problem is that you may be losing money on the work you are doing or just barely breaking even. The second problem is that you are most likely attracting cheap lawn care customers who only want cheap service. Cheap customers tend to not want any upsells and they are usually your biggest complainers.

As you try to apply this concept to commercial property maintenance there is a tendency to exacerbate the problem. Larger properties will bring larger estimate amounts and more work. You may find yourself so fixated on the dollar value of the bid that you fail to calculate your actual costs. You may also find yourself buying larger commercial equipment and then having to hire a staff. Not bringing in the proper amount of money on your commercial bids has brought on the ruin of many a lawn care business.

Some commercial property managers know this is a problem and they hate signing up a lawn care maintenance company at the beginning of the year only to have them go out of business half way through the year. They also won't go simply with the lowest bid, because they want quality work.

One lawn care business owner wrote about this and said "I'm new at this business and I didn't think it would be this hard to get started. I get lots of calls for estimates, I give bids but I never seem to get any.

The jobs I have been bidding on have been commercial jobs. Some are luxury condos. The normal price for my area is $80 to $85 dollars a month on each unit. I bid $70 a month.

The condo property maintenance is handled by a condo association and they range from 24 units to 36 units. The way I found out it was $80 to $85 a unit was by asking some guys that have been maintaining the property for years. They condo association has told me they received cheaper estimates but then they said (we go for the best service not the best price.) That's what they say and then end up not giving me work. I can't understand what else I should be doing."

A second lawn care business owner responded "It's good that you are getting lots of calls. Your advertising must be working.

What are your customer's reactions when you give estimates? Is your price too high or do they say they will think about it and just never call you back?

There are many steps you must take in professional and effective lawn care estimating.

I will list two ideas.

1) Sell quality. Don't let potential customers pick someone else simply because your bid is a few dollars higher. Let them know that you do quality work and that you are dependable. Take your potential customers for tours of their lawns as you give estimates. Point out areas that you will pay special attention too and show them how you can make a dramatic improvement in their yard.

2) Be ready to work immediately. I have found when doing estimates if I have my equipment with me and I can work immediately they often say 'go ahead' right away. Once they see a quality job they almost always sign on as regular customers.

Knowing and following all these steps will greatly increase your acceptance ratio.

So remember, start small, scale up step by step. Build profits and gain an understanding of what you need to charge to make a profit. Only make the jump to commercial properties once you have a firm understanding of how to run your business based on servicing residential properties."

BUSINESS ADVICE

Lawn care business advice from a 20 year veteran.

Any lawn care business owner that can make it through their first year is going to learn from a wealth of experiences. When we research lawn care business failure rates, the toughest year seems to be the first one. But can you imagine how much you would learn after 20 years in business? We got lucky to hear some business insight from such a veteran on the Gopher Lawn Care Business Forum.

He shared with us "I have been servicing lawn care customers for over 20 years now and I have learned so many lessons over the years, some good ones & some not so good.

The first lessons, that stands out to me is to buy the best piece of equipment (mower) you can afford to from the start. Do not go so far as to finance your entire equipment line as this is very risky for any new business. Get one good piece of equipment at a time. Budget for additional equipment needed. Then add to your equipment line only if you can afford to. Make it a part of your schedule to frequent your local pawn shops, craigslist, yard sales etc. for small equipment like blowers, trimmers, edgers etc. Many good deals can be had through such avenues.

Rent equipment whenever possible for jobs that are not part of your day to day operations. Buying equipment that sits idle most of the year, does not benefit you and will become a drain on your resources. Not to mention it will not start when you have the occasion to use it. Such idle equipment will become a maintenance nightmare.

From equipment to the field to the office there are so many considerations that are overlooked or just not done. From the office aspect, those pesky little receipts you get from the gas stations etc. that are thermally printed, make a physical copy and attach the original receipt to it. In about 1 years time that receipt is going be faded to the point that it is unreadable. The IRS doesn't accept a blank receipt as a deduction and that receipt is your proof should you get audited. Making copies of the receipt also helps to prevent loss. Keep your receipts in individual folders marked accordingly (IE gas, meals, repairs etc.) This makes the accounting process much more organized and easier to understand for both you and your accountant.

If you do not have a copier, get an all in one printer, that will do what you need, copy, fax and print.

Use the lawn care business calculators available on the Gopher Forum. I wish something like this had been available to use when I first started out. These calculator do not cover all considerations in the bidding process for a job but do give a great starting point. Use them.

When it comes to growing your lawn care business from residential accounts to commercial one, a lot of issues can arise. My biggest hurdle when getting into commercial lawn care work was not having enough equipment and personnel to get the job done properly and efficiently. It takes time and experience to be in the position to take on a commercial accounts and service them properly. So don't just jump into a huge commercial property bid. Take it step by step and scale up the size you service.

You also need to make sure when you service commercial properties that you build a rapport with the property owner/manager and keep in contact with them. After getting the account, the easiest mistake you can make is also the worse one to do and that is to fade into the background by just showing up to the job. Showing up only to do the work and limiting your interaction with the customer only to sending an invoice is a quick way to lose your accounts. If you find yourself doing that, you are out of touch with your business and your customers. Customers who feel out of touch with their lawn maintenance provider will more easily switch to the lowest bidder when their maintenance contract ends.

So to sum up my advise in a nutshell, don't bite off more than you can chew. Stay within you work capability and don't misrepresent your capabilities."

How to boost your lawn care revenues another $1,000 per month.

Ever wish you had an extra $1,000 or two in your account each and every month but are unsure how to do it? Here are some great ideas, from the Gopher Lawn Care Business Forum on how to initially contact and work with property managers. Following some simple steps should make it fairly easy for you to get on their contact list to do jobs on demand. As we will see, such jobs can command a premium in price because of their time sensitive status."

One lawn care business owner wrote "when I first was looking to move into the area I now live in, I was reading the local newspaper and saw an ad for rental properties available by a local real estate company. So I picked up the phone and talked to the property manager. I didn't end up getting a place from them at the time of the call but I felt it was productive as I was able to work into the conversation that I operate my own lawn care business.

Further on down the road, I did eventually end up renting from the property manager. As we were talking, I told her that the lawn care operation that she had did a bad job. So she thought she would give me a try. I've been doing work for them ever since.

If you are looking for a way to get more work, you really should consider this. The property manager is the person who is in charge of all the rental properties, like apartments and townhouses. Since I initially got work from one because the previous lawn care operation was doing a bad job and I pointed it out, I now have repeated this process and found even more work.

Don't be concerned if you are a small one man show. I was at first and found they will work with you. During my early conversations with the first property manager I dealt with, I told her that I was only a one person crew so I would really appreciate it if they could ease me into the jobs. They said that wouldn't be a problem because they didn't want to give too many jobs at once.

So the lesson learned here is the importance of networking and of being honest with people. When you are honest, it really shows your respect for them and in turn, you usually get it back."

A second lawn care business owner shared "I have been doing work for a couple property management companies for years now as well. One of them manages 1,500 properties and they load me up with work. I average $2,500 to $3,000 per month from them (some months it's the only thing that keeps me afloat).

What I have found is that they get so busy that they don't have time to call a vendor and get the work set up, then call the owners to get approval, etc. So I always just try and save them a step and mention that 'I could get it cleaned up for you today, or tomorrow… Just get the approval and I will get it done.'

Also while I am working on properties for them, I will keep my eye out for anything else that could be done. For instance I was doing a yard clean-up for a turnover and noticed a downed Oak tree on the back property. I called the maintenance manager and told him I could remove it for $100. He said sure go ahead. It took me about 2 hours and I had it all cut up and got a 1/2 cord out of it. I then put the wood on craigslist and had it sold the next day for $150.

Sometimes I notice dangerous limbs hanging, etc. Anything that could be a liability is an easy job to get.

The way I first got in with them was by driving by one of their properties and noticing it in bad shape. I called their number and asked for the maintenance manager. I talked to her and said 'I was driving by your property at ….and I can get it whipped into shape for you today for $xx.' She told me to bring her my license and insurance and after that, I could get started. That was it!

It has been a great business relationship ever since."

A third lawn care business owner shared "just a note for those of you that don't do work for rental agents. I currently work for several of them. They usually need what ever work they call you for done the same day they call. Most of the time it is because they are going to show the property. The downside to this kind of work is that it can throw a wrench into your regular mowing schedule.

Usually I am maintaining the properties when they are empty. This does allow me to pick up a new client from the renter a lot of times if I follow up with them. Such work can really add up too. Last year for me, these single one time jobs accounted for an average of about $500 to $700 in additional income per month. This year I estimate it to be much higher. They pay like clock work most of the time.

One of the reasons they will stick with you is not the price. Price is not the top priority for the agent since the owner pays for it. Instead, it is response time. They get paid when the property is rented or sold, so if they have someone to see the property they need you to get it looking its best asap for them. This is why they use you, it's your quick response time. When you give your price, make sure it is a little higher than the standard residential customer, to make it worth the inconvenience in scheduling."

Why you shouldn't rush growth on your lawn care business.

Most lawn care business owners tend to want to get their landscaping business big and as soon as possible. They see no downside to such growth and instead only think of what they feel are all the positive things that come along with growing larger. Yet when you get a chance to talk to a lawn care business owner who has been there and done that, you see a very different opinion on fast growth. A member of the Gopher Lawn Care Business Forum shared with us his experiences on it and how it hurt his business.

He wrote "hello, I am the owner of a grounds maintenance business that has been in operation for 15 years. I feel like an old timer in the lawn cutting world even though I am only 35 years old. I have been through a lot and seen a lot at the same time.

I was a one man operation for my first 8 years, then I decided, enough was enough and I wanted to grow as large as possible. When I made the decision to go big, I did get to the point of having 3 trucks and 9 employees. One day I was mowing one of my large apartment complexes and found that I truly hated it.

The business totally changed for me. I found there was way too much b.s. and ass kissing involved to keep the work. When I came to this realization, I thought to myself that I had been running a lawn care business for too long up to that point to have to operate in such a manner to keep work. I felt I just didn't need it and I hated the fact that I was hating my own business. It was insanity! My creation turned into a monster and what was once a thing that I owned now became something that owned me!

So I decided to make a change once again. I slowly let work and employees go until I was back to just working by myself. I found I was much, much happier that way. I felt like I was back to loving my business again and I was getting up in the morning with a smile on my face, ready to go to work. In order to keep things more fresh and keep my mind working, I decided to branch out and begin offering landscaping services.

As I look back now, there are some things I would have done differently. First off, I would not tried to grow so fast. When I started marketing to commercial lawn care customers, they seemed to come on fast, too fast. I got 4 luxury apartment complexes, with the smallest being 14 acres and ranging all the way up to 22 acres for the largest, all within a 4 month period. On top of those customers, I had to continue to service all my residential lawn care customers along with some smaller commercial properties.

I always felt like I was a loyal person to my loyal customers but over time my attention to detail with those residential customers went down the drain. Instead of paying attention to the customers who really mattered most to me and did the most for me, I was constantly driving around to all the large commercial lawn care customers, doing damage control and kissing property managers' butts because of the crappy job my crews were doing.

I personally lost the love for the work. That really was a big downer for me personally. So if I could offer any advice to other lawn care business owners out there, it would be to go slow and don't try to grow big too soon. Add services to your business that you enjoy. Don't add them all at once either. Do it one at a time. Learn how to perform the service the best way you know how and then add another service. Also, find TRUSTED, HARD WORKING people to work for you. That's a lot tougher than it sounds. But most of all, don't lose your love for the work. As long as you want to get up in the morning to go to work, do it the best you can and you will feel proud when you come home at night."

Answers to newbie lawn care business owner questions.

Any new lawn care business owner is most certainly going to have a lot of questions about running their business. Here are a few questions that came up on the Gopher Lawn Care Business Forum from a new lawn care business owner who was having some difficulties getting started. Below each question are some answers from veteran lawn care business owners.

He wrote "wow, this is a wonderful forum with so much information. My new lawn care business has three partners. We are all under or unemployed and NEED to work. We are interested in the lawn care business, have lots of personal experience with our own yards and in dealing with lawn care companies as consumers. We have the essential equipment to start, such as mowers, edgers, trimmers, truck, trailer. We have the determination to make it work and the willingness to learn. Out of the three of us, I am the researcher who will be trying to digest as much information as I can over time. Tonight I've been reading up on advertising - suggestions on signs, flyers, business cards, social networking, google maps, craigslist, etc. I also have found invaluable information on calculating base hourly rates for job estimates.

Right now this is where we are at. We have come up with a company name, slogan, and colors. We have a tax id number and a DBA with the state. We have a dress code. We don't have a logo. We don't have a lot of cash to start up with for professional signs, flyers, post cards, etc. But we want to be as professional as possible with what we have.

My questions at the moment are:

1. Would you say it is smart to start with one 'free demo' home in a large neighborhood (it's a friend) to show our quality of work and display a sign in the front yard?"

Of course! Advertise in any way possible. You might have neighbors bugging you for service in no time. I recommend getting business cards, you can write estimates on the back & it makes you seem professional. It's better than handing them a piece of paper.

"2. Is it ok to start out with basic magnetic do-it-yourself signs for the truck ($20 for 2 at Staples), home-made yard signs made from plywood, do-it-yourself flyers and business cards?"

Yes sir! As a new company I wouldn't recommend anything more. In the future, you will probably want to change the look & keeping your signs costs down now will allow you do to this without regretting how much you had initially spent on them before you knew what you really wanted. After you feel more comfortable that you want to continue with your business, professional permanent signs for your trucks should be your next goal.

"3. How do you go about bidding on commercial contract mowing jobs? Or finding out about them?"

In my area, unless you carry at least $1,000,000.00 in liability insurance, you probably don't stand a chance and no commercial customer would even consider using your services! To find them, you need to ask around. You need to network with people and this starts with people you already know because most everyone you know works somewhere and knows other people that work at other locations. All of these people will have contacts and can refer you. You also need to create a referral system. Offer your current customer something in exchange for each customer they bring you. The best way to get people interested in you, is to speak with them face to face, sell yourself in person.

"4. How do you approach businesses such as shopping centers, apartment complexes, etc?"

Visit each location and find out who is in charge of property maintenance. You will most likely have to ask for the property manager. Talk to that person. Find out when they accept bids and remember to submit a bid when they ask. Follow up after you submit your bid to see what they thought of it. It also never hurts to go into a meeting prepared with an estimate in hand for lawn care services. That way you could swoop up the account right there on the spot.

"5. Is it too late in spring to get a new lawn care business started?"

It's never too late to get your lawn care business started. Tons of people are hiring lawn care businesses now because they now see the grass growing. In panic, you might get hired instantly & be expected to work immediately. Try advertising to lawns with uncut grass.

"6. How do you go about finding low-cost and quality sources of fertilizers, mulches, top soil, etc."

Google, yellow pages, etc. Call companies and ask around. I have found great interest in organic lawn care products. They might be a little more expensive, but they are concentrated, easy to mix & apply, and easy to sell.

"7. How do we find out about all of the licenses that we need to get?"

Visit your township, county and state government websites and search for professional licenses. Most of the time you won't need a license for lawn care but you will probably need one for landscaping.

"8. You know how some business cards will say 'bonded and insured'? What is that and do you really need it?

You will need liability insurance but most likely you won't need to be bonded unless a commercial or government account requires it. The surety bond would be purchased through an insurance company. Very basically, the bond agrees to make good the default or debt you would owe a customer if you failed to perform your services in the manner you agreed to perform them.

Building your business on commercial or residential lawn care customers, what's better?

This topic always makes for a lively debate on the Gopher Lawn Care Business Forum. Should you build your lawn care business on commercial lawn care customers or residential customers and why? The answer a lot of times is shaped by the experience each business owner has had with these different types of customers. However when everything settles down, some common points seem to become clear and one path seems to stand out as a better way to go.

One lawn care business owner asked "I have built my business with about 95% residential lawn care clients and have done a few big commercial lawn care bids in the past week or so (still no word on if I got them or not). But to be honest I kinda hope I don't get them & may turn them down if I do. It seems to me everybody out there wants the big commercial lawn mowing jobs so badly that it's extremely cut throat and not worth it.

Say for example there is a 5 acre commercial property. Everybody wants that big contract so bad that the going rate seems to be $9,000-$10,000 a year. If you break it down, it has much lower profit margins than an already competitive residential market! My average residential area lot is 10,000 SF. So in terms of square footage 5 acres is equal to approx. 22 residential lots. What I make going out & servicing 22 lawns in day (which is about what I do daily) is nearly what these commercial contracts pay per month!

So I ask the guys who focus on commercial properties….. What gives? If I can go out with 1 helper & in a day (16 total labor hours) make almost as much on residential as a big commercial property pays for a month (that would take 2 guys, a half day, 4 times a month = 2 days = 32 total labor hours). Why the hell does anyone do it? If you were just starting out & needed the work I could see it, but the companies that focus towards this are usually well established.... I just don't get it? I can't get passed that what I make mowing 22 residential properties monthly is over a grand more per month than these places are paying for the same square footage. I'm not hurting for work by any means (thank god) and I don't 'need' these jobs.

I get calls from my advertising for commercial jobs, so I go & bid them. What the heck right? I look at them several ways.... by sq footage, by time, accounted for the fact that one big account means less travel, fuel, even oil changes & brakes.... Still I don't see it. I bid the jobs a decent bit over what they are currently paying but still less than what I think it's worth to me really so as I said earlier.... I'm not gonna cry either way over these. I just hope maybe somebody can help shed a little light as to maybe a big advantage I'm not seeing here? I consider myself more intelligent than the average idiot but maybe I'm looking at this from the wrong angle?"

A couple of other lawn care business owners told us why they liked commercial lawn care accounts.

One said "the benefits are small in size, but add up. Like for instance you said less gas, travel time, etc. You also have to take into account there are less people to deal with (sometimes residential customers can take up a ton of your time by chatting, or this and that). Then you are also sending out 1 bill instead of 20. It's less monthly paper work, and less stamps.

I think you do more in a day than most other companies. Where they may be servicing 10 residential customers in a day, half a day job would only replace 5 of them instead of your 10 or 12. So the pay seems better for them."

A second added "what I like about commercial mowing jobs is you can usually quote a bit higher, since the person taking bids for the job isn't the one paying you. They don't care what you charge, so they're not going to be offended if you bill them a bit higher. I've just taken on 3 commercial accounts, 2 at $300/month and one at $350/month. All I have to do is cut the grass twice a month (none of them take over 2 hours) and do a bit of weeding/other stuff maybe once every two months. It's a pretty sweet deal if you ask me."

And here is a view on why commercial lawn care accounts aren't the way to go.

One business owner shared "well, here is my 2 cents. Residential customers are the way to go. In the area I live, every pickup truck has a mower in the back. They go after these small commercial properties because the misconception is that they pay better. That might have been so in the past, but companies now are hiring people to cut costs. So they are going through contracts with a fine tooth comb.

With residential, as long as you have a good reputation, if you fall within $5 dollars of all the other bids, you're gonna get the job. I recently combined my crews and was able to downsize my cutting crew to three guys. They are cutting lawns and if everything goes smoothly and efficiently, I can make upwards of $8,000.00 a week. That's right!

With over 180 lawn care accounts to perform, my foreman just called and said they are done for the week. It's 10:30 on Friday morning. With those numbers, I can not see why I'd go underbid myself on a commercial property. In fact, even with this recession, I just gave all my guys a $1.00/hr raise across the board. It's all about efficiency with residential. My guys don't speak with the customer unless they have an issue that needs immediate attention, otherwise they call the office.

And to address the issue of billing, since we've switched to automated billing, we bill out over $3,500.00 of weekly lawn service every Sunday. Payroll capital is never an issue now. And it cost a little less than invoicing with paper and stamps. My advice is to keep tightening your residential lawn care customer routes and know your limits. Take a map of the area that you do work in and create geographic boundaries. If you do this, you will make money!!!!"

What are you training your lawn care employees to do?

When you hire employees for your lawn care business, they are on the front lines and the impressions they make with the public and your customer base is going to do a lot to effect whether your business survives or fails. So think about these things when you are considering what you are training your lawn care employees.

Do you have a sales manager for your lawn care business? One business owner wrote "I am in the process of hiring a sales manager to where I will be able to work with them on contacting homeowner associations. I also want them to go to other businesses that could be connected to us, like lawn mower repair shops, real estate agents, builders, mortgage companies, etc. to work with them on sending us referrals.

With my mowing crews, I am training them to be the first to say hi to people while they are out and about. This is very important to me as they are the ambassadors of my business. They need to come across as approachable and friendly.

My lawn care crews are also trained to look for problems in the customer's lawn, not just mow the lawn and go. If the customer is not home, they will write a note on their invoice recommending a specific product/treatment. Our lawn care technicians always go to the door and knock before doing any treatment. If the customer is home they will see if there is anything specific they want them to look at.

Keep these ideas in mind as your lawn care business grows and you look for ways to help your staff bring in more business. They are on the front lines and are in the best position to offer suggestions and upsells to your lawn care customer which ultimately brings in more profits."

A printer shares his business and marketing insights.

Do you ever wish you could ask what your competitors are doing with their marketing? What about business questions to help you find out what makes some businesses successful while others fail? A member on the Gopher Lawn Care Business Forum shared with us some of his fascinating business insight. He is a printer and helps many lawn care business owners get their marketing material designed, printed, and shipped. He has seen a lot of what works and what doesn't. So I asked him a bunch of business questions.

He introduced himself by saying "Hello, I own a printing company that I started in 1999 and have over 20 years of printing experience. Right now I do printing for over 30 landscaping businesses in my area. I design and print flyers, doorhangers, forms, envelopes, letterheads, business cards also design logos for them."

With all your printing experience, have you found landscapers or lawn care professionals tend to choose one marketing method over another? For instance, do they prefer, door hangers, flyers, or postcards? What is your view on which marketing method works best?

He replied "flyers with pictures seem to be the most popular item with lawn care businesses. You want to have a good looking flyer with coupons. Most of my landscapers use two color flyers because of the cheap price."

What advice do you have for new start up businesses? You have been in business now for many years and must have seen a lot. Where do you think that most tend to trip up and how can they avoid those problems?

"Most businesses fail because either they don't attract a sufficient number of new customers, or they let their existing or current customers slip away. If you really want your business to be successful, you've got to make getting and keeping customers your number one priority.

Let me put it another way. When was the last time you heard of a company going out of business because they had too many happy, satisfied customers buying from them? My guess is, never!

On the other hand, you can probably name quite a few businesses that are no longer around because they didn't have enough people buying from them, coming back for more and referring others to them.

And that's where marketing comes in. Marketing is the ability to get your message out to others about the goods and services you offer, in such a manner that it compels them... nearly forces them to do business with you. It is one of the most fundamental, yet misunderstood areas in business today. Also most businesses don't look at marketing as an investment to grow their business and a tax write-off.

Effective marketing is critical to the success of any business. With ineffective marketing, your prospects may never find out about the products or services you offer."

When it comes to keeping customers, what have you found that keeps them around?

Also do you find the marketing message trying to attract new customers is different from trying to keep current customers?

"CUSTOMER SERVICE!!!

Everyone is in the business of customer satisfaction. The purpose of a business is to create and keep a customer. All business activities must be focused on this central purpose.

You keep customers by delivering on your promises, fulfilling your commitments and continually investing in the quality of your relationships. If your job is customer satisfaction, your real job title is problem-solver. Offer your customers a long-term relationship, then do everything possible to build and maintain it."

Snow plowing business basics.

As summer turns to fall and fall turns to winter I am seeing a lot more questions on how to get your snow plowing business started. How do you get customers? What's better, residential or commercial snow plowing? This is a topic that was brought up on the Gopher Lawn Care Business Forum and I wanted this information pointed out.

What's the best way to get snow plowing customers?

A snow plowing business owner wrote "sending letter to managers of commercial facilities will work, however the return is small from what we have found. If you want to pick up some commercial snow plow accounts, first you're going to want to target your lawn accounts… Next start cold calling / knocking on doors etc… Start calling mangers, stopping in, and talking to them.

Ask them if they're happy with their current snow removal provider and if they're taking bids this year.

Keep in mind:

1. Always try to set up a meeting with them… Talk to them find out what they want.

2. Put together a bid packet.

3. Drop a bid packet back off to them.

* The above should be all done within a 48hour time frame.

4. Send them a thank you card afterward. We send them the same day we meet/drop our bid off.

5. Do a check up call if you don't hear anything within 7 days.

6. Don't sit back and wait for the phone to ring."

Another lawn care business owner followed up with this question "this subject has been haunting me for a while now. Not only is snow removal a good income earner but, as far residential snow removal goes is it worth it?

For a one person operation you have 20 accounts. That's 20 hours by yourself as well as drive time in the snow. Plus fuel and we all know you use more fuel in the winter months. Everybody who has been laid off or unemployed now seems to be doing snow removal. What's the rates for residential? I live in a cold state. North Dakota and it snows almost daily. Blizzards and drifts and below zero atmospheres that make you wonder what you are doing here. -40 to -60 .

I live in an apartment and this snow plowing company is in front of the building I live at and he never did the snow removal here. I know the guy who did. He is offering $100 a month snow removal. So let's go back to what I said, you have 20 accounts at $100 a month. That's what, 2 grand a month? If it snows more then 3 times a week your sucking air… and you are losing $$$. If it doesn't snow and you have 20 people and they are paying you $100 a month they're going to want to be compensated and it does happen. A contract is merely a written statement. Are you really going to take someone to small claims court because they didn't want to pay $100 for no service? I don't know what to think, that's where I am at with it. Is this lowballer making money?"

Another responded "a snow plowing company up here in my neck of the woods only does driveways.

When you do all the math they were only charging like $11 ish a push… But they were charging a seasonal push and their service area was only 10 miles from there shop…. So they had a real tight route.

They made around $400K a year on plowing drive ways and when you break that down by the hour, they were doing around $100 per hour per truck which is going rate for this area…

So by the hour he was doing good, but if you look at him by the push $11 a drive is pretty damn low.

So what am I saying? Most may say that they lowball cause the $11 price…. but in my book you have to look at your hourly rate more than anything."

SALES ADVICE

How to get your first commercial lawn care customer.

If you are a newer lawn care business owner who hasn't made the jump yet to servicing commercial properties, you might be thinking, how do I land my first commercial lawn care bid. This questions seems to come up often and when I hear stories from those who made the leap I love to pass them on to you to help.

One of the members of the Gopher Lawn Care Business Forum wrote about his experience. "On a whim I just bid and won my first commercial job....

I noticed a really overgrown commercial property for sale and thought they may not have someone to take care of it. I was right and they were getting complaints from neighbors. My time estimate for the job was right on so the job went well.

Now, if I want to continue, I know I need to invest in better tools of the trade. Thanks to the Gopher Forum for the information and templates, I followed one of them for my quote.

The job is for a former steakhouse, about the size of an Olive Garden. I learned that I can do the job with basic equipment and techniques but better tools would make it easier and faster.

IMHO I bid it perfectly. I ended up a half hour shy of my estimated time. I spoke to a friend that has an established lawn care business and he told me he would have done it for the same but he would have done it for less if he needed the work.

The restaurant is closed and the property is up for lease/sale. The owner is unsure if he will raze it or remodel.

Here is how I won this job:

1. I noticed a property for sale that is lacking attention.
2. I called the realtor listed on the sign and ask to service the property.
3. The realtor took my info, actually I emailed it to him.
4. Realtor passed info along to property owner.
5. Property owner's assistant contacted me and requested a quote.
6. I then had to find a suitable format for a quote (that I got from the forum), I took another look at the property, visualized the work and put the quote in my own format.
7. In the meantime the realtor contacted me and pressed me to get the quote in…the neighbors were complaining about the weeds.
8. I submitted my quote after settling on what I thought was a fair wage for my estimated time and materials.
9. The owner emailed me directly and accepted the quote, his assistant also emailed me and asked for a start date which I made a priority.
10. I completed the job quickly, took pics and, using a template, created an invoice which I then emailed to the asst.
11. I contacted the realtor to let him know the job was complete. I also requested that he contact me when similar services are needed. He replied that he would and that I should keep in touch.

I see a niche market for servicing commercial properties w/o a long term contract…especially with businesses failing and new business growth stalled. A lot of properties are on hold and will fall into a state of disrepair w/o care."

What great advice and simple steps to take in order to submit a bid to a commercial property owner. I hope these ideas help you land more commercial properties as well.

How a new lawn care business landed commercial accounts.

A very popular question many new lawn care business owners ask is how can they land commercial accounts. A business owner on the Gopher Lawn Care Business Forum was kind enough to share some of his insights with us. He wrote "I started my lawn care business 2 months ago with 5 customers. As of today I have 18 residential and 3 commercial customers.

Landing commercial accounts can be tough, however I have found that getting your information out there can be a big help. One of my secrets to getting one of my commercial accounts was just sitting back and letting the other lawn service guys do my work for me.

When I first started getting my lawn care business going this spring, I was becoming frustrated because every place I went to market my business already had one of the other lawn services and had used them for a few seasons. I was getting pretty discouraged. Until it dawned on me one day. Heck, these other lawn service guys are pretty much doing my work for me! I started noticing that their quality of work was really lax. They were mowing lawns when it was really wet, leaving tracks and huge unsightly clumps of grass all over. It was obvious they weren't keeping their blades sharp on their mowers because they were missing spots all over. And the thing that shocked me the most was they weren't even trimming! At all! It really looks like hell when you don't trim around the electrical poles, service boxes, and even curbs near the highways and streets.

Now I admit, sometimes you can get away with skipping a trim job here and there, but only when it isn't going to be obvious from a block away (literally!) These commercial businesses rely on a professional appearance (much like we do) and they want a nice neatly trimmed lawn, much like what was promised to them in their pricing when their lawn service bid it to them. The way I see it, these guys are just setting themselves up for someone like me to come along and say, 'hey I can do the same service for the same price, but I'll actually live up to my promises.' Now, yes, this is probably a good way to make some lawn services pretty upset, however my answer to that is if you are doing your job right, I should be no threat to you.

Now one of my commercial accounts was obtained because I went to all the local real estate offices and dropped off my door hanger with my business card stapled to it. It just so happened that one of the realtor's clients had 6 buildings behind the real estate office in the same complex that had it's previous lawn service go out of business. So the owner had called the real estate business and asked if they knew of anybody who did lawn service. Most of the agents don't have a particular business in mind when they recommend someone, so she just grabbed my information and passed it on. I was the only lawn care business that had cards there.

Now that was just luck, not something you'd really learn in business school, but hey, it worked for me and I continue to stop by these offices frequently and ask if they need anymore business cards. It lets them know you are proactive with your business and if you make small talk with some of the agents every time, you make friends and next thing you know, they are recommending you over the other guys..great P.R.! It's just human nature to hire someone you know a little about rather than just a name in a phone book.

Aside from the graphics on my truck, my best way to attract new customers is by word of mouth. I offer a free mowing for every new referred customer that signs up for the entire season. Something else I learned from the templates on the Gopher

Forum!

One last word of advice:
When you service someone's lawn, or perform any service for that matter, don't just try to do it as fast as you possibly can and then move on to the next job. Yes, speed and efficiency is a good thing. BUT, take some time to visit with your customer. Get to know them, their needs, and their concerns. Ask them how their vacation went or how the family is. You'd be surprised how fast you'll get referrals when they realize you're human and not just like the machine you operate all day. You also gain trust, which is HUGE in the referral process. Next thing you know, you're not just servicing the old lady across from your other account, your servicing her family and her family's neighbors, and their neighbors too. Word of mouth can be a wonderful thing. Let it work to your advantage!"

How to get commercial lawn care accounts, without commercial references.

Before you make the jump from residential customers to commercial customers, ask yourself why you want to do this. Many lawn care business owners would suggest taking a few years to get your footing in the business world before making the jump from residential customers to commercial. The vast majority of commercial accounts will take the longest of your customer base to pay you. They will use up most of your resources to service them. They will be looking for the cheaper of the bid prices. Most will require proof of insurance as well. If after reading this warning, you are still ready to take the jump, continue reading. We don't want to discourage you, we do however want to give you a heads up before you act.

In 1961 Joseph Heller wrote a novel entitled 'Catch-22.' It is about a WWII era bombardier who's Colonel keeps raising the number of missions a flight crew must take part in order to complete their service. Yossarian, the bombardier, wants to get out of these missions. He thinks he finds a bureaucratic rule that will get him out. The rule states, a soldier is considered insane if he continues to fly dangerous combat missions. However, it continues, if a soldier files a formal request stating he is insane because of flying such missions, the very act of doing so states you are sane. Thus the catch-22.

We recently had been asked the following question which could be viewed as another example of a catch-22.

One lawn care business owner wrote "my company is currently trying to expand into the commercial arena, meaning condominium complexes, apartment complexes, and other such buildings. We are trying to convince property managers to accept our bids for the landscape maintenance of their properties. Our problem we have been running into is that we don't have any experience in the commercial field. For the last few years we have been servicing only residential properties. Without any commercial references all the property managers that we have dealt with refuse to accept our bids. But if we can't get any commercial properties to service, how will we ever have any experience. My question is, what do you think would be a good way to sell our services even though we lack commercial experience."

What a great question! We asked some of our friends in the industry to shed light on this problem and how to break out of this never ending loop.

A second lawn care business owner shared "to overcome this, I initially put together a professional portfolio and went to all the local home owner association board meetings. I let them know that I can offer something more for their property, and I showed them my knowledge of botany and horticulture. It is all about presentations, right down to how your write your proposals/quotes and contract specifications.

When you know a property is out for tender, bid on it and show interest. Let them know a five year plan, and how you can improve the current landscape, even if it's just by implementing a weed control and fertilizing program.

Property managers don't rely on experience (most of the time) they want someone that can adapt to their ways. You might be working for the property manager, but they are working for hundreds of people, at just one address."

A third business owner suggested to get your start with small commercial properties.

"If you have any friends, relatives that work at a small commercial building see if you can get some kind of reference to do the job. I was also asked about references from commercial properties early on when all I had was residential accounts. I told them I had been doing it for a while, worked for other companies servicing commercial accounts, and have just started out on my own. I gave them the choice to sign a two week agreement so they could get a feel for the kind of work I do before being committed to a full year.

I also suggest you take pictures of bigger residential jobs you work on and show them to potential commercial jobs. I guess just sell yourself, show confidence that you can perform good quality work."

A fourth shared "from my own experience I have found that most larger clients want someone with a proven background in large properties. As stated by others, you need to start with the smaller commercial properties and build a client base and resume. My company specializes in large retail complexes and apartment complexes now. But we didn't start there. We first did banks, restaurants, retail stores and similar sites that were under 1 acre in size.

You just can't expect an owner to hand over a contract for services worth $30,000 or higher to someone who has never done anything larger than a $50 lawn cut. They want to be sure that the contractor will have the experience, manpower and equipment to handle a job of this size. We all have to start at the bottom and work our way up.

You can get your foot in the door with the 'low-end' commercial accounts by knowing your residential customers a bit. Odds are you have customers on their Home Owner Association board, customers that are in decision-making roles at their jobs, customers that are also business owners. If you let them know you're looking to get into the commercial market, they might be more than happy to give you a shot.

So all this shows you how important it is to start small at first but how do you do that?

1. Networking. This is a scary term for some, but it means that you use every contact you can think of to get a job! If you have friends or family, you have a job that's yours for the asking. My brother works in the offices of a machine shop. I just asked him to see if his boss would accept a bid. Now I'm cutting the lawn. Who cuts the grass where your family works? Are they part of a HOA? Kid brother who waits tables at a local restaurant? The guy who cuts your hair? The gas station near your house? Does your accountant have an office building? Your dentist? The list is endless. IF you start writing a list of contacts you know, and where they work (small places are best) you'll come up with an impressive list of opportunities. Very few small companies will turn down the offer for you to submit a bid. What do they have to lose?

2. Once you get a handful of these jobs and prove yourself, contact the decision-maker and ask if they've been happy with their service. I assume the answer will be yes. Then all you need to do is thank them for their business and ask if it'd be okay to list them as a reference. Why would anyone say no? Now you have experience and references.

3. Now you go into an industrial park with tons of small businesses. Some small, some large. Send a letter addressed to 'maintenance dept.' Even if they don't have one, they'll get it to the right person. Simply send them a letter describing your company and services. Tell them you'll be in the area next season, and may I submit a bid. Put a tear-off on the letter where they can

answer 'Yes, please submit a bid….and give a place for name and phone.' And, put the box there for them to check off 'No, we're not interested in looking for a better service provider at this time.' Most people, like me, hate cold calling. You'll get plenty of people willing to accept a bid. It might cost you a few bucks in postage (I would include a return envelope). But, lawn care is usually last on the business owner's mind. Don't ask for a phone conversation or face to face quite yet. They have other things to attend to. The letter is not an 'in your face sales pitch' and leaves an opportunity to say no. People will be interested from your letter, and they'll give you a name and number to call. This prevents you from wasting time trying to get by secretaries, and harassing people who don't want to talk. There's plenty of work out there….go after those who want to talk with you!"

A fifth business owner added "in order to sell large commercial accounts or what we call (HVCP) meaning Highly Visible Commercial Properties, you first need a photo on a postcard displaying your equipment line (fleet of mowing equipment) along with your employee's and a bit of info about your company.

Second, you need to follow up and follow up some more. Touch base and re-touch base. You need to litter the city with your signs. Don't be afraid to continue to call upon them year after year. It usually takes six times of talking with someone before they are willing to meet with you.

Third, know your stuff, meaning your industry. Just a little bit of turf grass knowledge will put you leaps and bounds above the common competitor.

Lastly, become a full lawn service. These type of clients you are going after need someone with extensive knowledge in areas of sprinkler systems, lawn care, shrubbery work, lawn maintenance and snow plowing. If you don't or can't provide these services get there, because if these clients are your hope for the future then you need the above skills."

A sixth business owner wrote "I've been thinking about the mowing part of business and where I'd like to go with it and I think I have something in mind…Now all I have to do is figure out how to go about making it a reality.

After talking with people and seeing some other companies plus knowing my personal preference, I've come to realize that I'd like to get larger properties for mowing. I personally like the larger properties because you're at one spot for a while instead of a constant stop/go every 30 minutes and I just like being out by myself for hours at a time! Plus it cuts down costs due to being at one location longer. I talked to a couple companies that do mostly large properties and have a few smaller profitable residential accounts just to fill in time. One company in particular only does churches and that interested me. From my experience, churches are pretty laid back on requirements but they don't go looking for bids every year like commercial properties do (trying to save money), they just let them come in.

So checking out the area we have a lot of churches here. On one of the main roads in my township alone has seven of them. One of them is the church I attend and they're the largest but they're out because some guy underbid it and locked himself into a three year contract or until he folds up. Now I'm just trying to think of the best way to present myself to these churches and get my name in there in an attempt to put bids on them in the fall or whenever they will accept bids. I'm thinking a good letter with brochure that showcases the company would be a good starting point.

Points of interest to them would be professional service, insured/state certified for herbicides/fertilizers, starting to specialize in larger properties, competitive rates due to being efficient. So I'd highlight all those features in a brochure and have pictures of the equipment and me.

Another big factor in why I'd like to do this is, I'd still be able to easily turn $60 per man hour gross, even with an employee, and the only other equipment I'd need is one more mower. I already have the 60″ with an efi engine and that thing does a heck of a workload so I'd probably add a 72″ with an efi engine or a diesel when I would step up to having to hire someone.

Now I wouldn't be limiting myself to churches alone, I'd move to condo associations too and even go for commercial properties that have good size lots. Basically I'm trying to go for the end of mowing that requires being more of an actual company and being more professional, attempting to get away from the tons of mow & go companies.

I talked with a guy yesterday that mows only large properties (15 acres and up) and he makes a very good living with it. He gave me some suggestions on how to get my name in the door with the places I'm interested in. I thought about sending the letters out, but he said he's never had luck with letters and the best way to do it is go right in and ask for the property manager or the person in charge of the grounds maintenance. He said to make little binders that show all your credentials and some pictures of work/equipment, and a description of the company and it's benefits to the customer. Go in, introduce yourself and give them the binder and ask to be placed on their list for bids.

So that's going to be my next project, make the binders up. I'm already starting a list of properties that I'll give them out to. When I break it down, the odds look a lot better. Not many companies can or want to service larger places around here, I think there is about 5-8 companies that I see servicing all the larger properties. Then when you figure out how many properties there are compared to those few of guys. Also when you factor in that I could fill a 6 day mowing schedule for 2 guys with about 20-25 large properties compared to 120 residential homes, that also means better odds of filling up a schedule quick.

Here is the breakdown of the presentation binders I use. It has a cover sheet which has the company logo and number. Then 2 pages that describes the business and it's advantages. Next page has copies of my fertilizer certification, business license, proof of insurance. Then a thank you page, basically thanking them for taking the time to read it and to keep us in mind when they're looking for bids. I'm going to have a few pictures scattered in the first page and maybe one or two in the thank you page just to help fill it out and show off a little."

Wow! Now that is some amazingly insightful information for those who are making the jump from servicing residential properties to commercial. By taking this powerful information from these business owners in the know, you can get your company to break out of this catch-22.

Ideas on how your lawn care business can sell better.

Are you looking for more ways to improve your sales skills? A member of the Gopher Lawn Care Business Forum shared with us some of his sales secrets. He wrote "I have 7 years of sales experience in retail and business. What got me to start my lawn care business was one day when I was speaking to my neighbor about getting loam and seeds for his front yard and I told him I could do it and gave him a quote. He liked and accepted it. So I did the math and my profit was only $300.00. Yes that's for a day but I wanted more. Am I greedy? Yes, but that's what makes the world go round. So I used my sales skills and up sold him a retaining wall, plants, landscape lighting as well as a walkway. Now my profit was higher and he was happy.

To improve your sales skills, the first thing I would suggest is do not offer the sale, ask for it. What I mean by this is, don't say 'oh I can buy mulch and lay it and spread it for you if you'd like.' Instead say 'I noticed you need mulch over there because the rain washed most of it away. When would you like me to place the order for you? It will cost …..' Then the customer will think 'hmm, well you're the professional, saying that I need it. So can we get it today or tomorrow?'

Another thing to consider is compliments help in your sales pitch. You might want to say things like 'oh Mr. Johnson I love your front yard and house. I would love to own such a nice house & yard like yours.' Customers love when you compliment their house. If you do that and build trust with them, you will have a client who will keep calling you and tell their friends about you.

I have done jobs where I was in sales before and I have learned how to read and talk to people. My all time favorite thing to do is to upsell. Say you get a call about an ad you placed online or in the local newspaper. You go over to their home or business and estimate it. Don't forget to compliment the potential customer by saying 'you have a nice house Mrs. Smith, you know a nice slate walkway with some pretty flowers and lights along it would be great for curb appeal.' The next thing you will see is the customer looking to you to tell them how much it will cost.

I do my own marketing and I have found that sending flyers through the mail doesn't work. So instead I ordered a shirt and some business cards, to better improve the image I am projecting to others. I also go door to door. I have some public places that let me place some flyers in their store along with my business cards.

The biggest marketing mistake I see others do is leaving a crummy black and white flyer or a flyer that is boring at someone's door. A boring flyer would be one that uses a title line like 'We Offer Great Deals.' Everyone and their grandmother use such a title line. What I do instead on my flyers is I say 'Don't Let Your Lawn Fall Into Disrepair, Call The Team That Can Make Your Dreams Come True' or 'We Work For You And Your Lawn Why Wait? Call Today.' I will also put catchy pictures and words on my flyers.

Not only is marketing a good way to get sales but having knowledge about the landscaping field is important as well. If you were hiring a crew to mow your lawn and build a retaining wall, you would want the lawn care business owner to be knowledgeable about their field. Knowledge is very important. I have explained to my neighbors and friends a problem with something in their lawn and then I follow it up by telling them how I could fix it. I will point things out like how to remove crab grass or how to install an irrigation system.

What helps in this department is to STUDY STUDY STUDY. You might think you know everything, but you need to realize you don't. You need to read every night about landscaping and watch how to videos. I listen and watch how to videos to see how they do things. I also get ideas and learn new ways to explain things to customers. I recently landed a $10,000 contract for a condo association because I knew what I was talking about and how to present it. Because of that, the association president liked me.

Some of the other things I am doing to promote my lawn care business is to place flyers in a local pizzeria. I went back 3 days later to get a drink and check on the flyers and they were all gone. The owner told me that people were taking them left and right. I am also working with realtors in my area to get added to their contact database. If someone is buying or selling a house and is in need of a landscaper to add curb appeal to their property or clean the area up, they now know they can call me to help.

I put the time spent driving around town to good use. When I am out driving around during the day I look around to see what residential or commercial properties are for sale. Then I will call the realtor phone number listed on the sign, and let them know I am available any time they have a yard that needs to be cleaned up or landscaped. I will also point out any issues I see on the property that is for sale and tell them how I can correct the problem.

Try some of these tips out and you will see an improvement in your sales."

How to upsell snow removal services.

The way you present your snow plowing bid can have a direct impact on whether or not you get hired and what kinds of services your customer will sign up for. I asked a member of the Gopher Lawn Care Business Forum about his methods for estimating snow removal services and how he gets so many upsells. He told me of the importance of breaking down each service in your bid to show the cost of each. Then I followed up with more questions.

How often do your customers go for the bare bones snow plow job versus want you to take care of everything? Are you ever able to upsell them when they want to go for the cheapest? If so, what do you suggest a snow plow operator say to help increase the dollar value of the sale?

He responded by saying "most customer have told me they like the way I break down the pricing & accept the whole package. This way they see what their money is paying for. Say you tell Mr. B, who has an average sized lot but a big wrap around sidewalk & wants de-icer, it will cost him $50 each snowfall. Now lets say he knows that Mr. X next door to him is only paying $35 & has a bigger lot. You just lost a customer. He doesn't realize Mr. X only has a front door & no sidewalks at all.

Business owners usually only think of it as 'snowplowing the lot.' They don't look at the big picture regardless of the services they want. Now let's say it this way: snow removal of the lot is $30 (less then MR. X, he'll like that), 'you have a pretty big sidewalk' snow removal for it will be $15, you also want de-icer that will be $20. Then you tell him 'I'll use a broadcast spreader that will cover your sidewalk & a little bit of the parking spaces along the sidewalk.' BINGO! He thinks he just got a deal. He's paying less then Mr. X for 'snowplowing' and he's getting a larger area de-iced than he had planned. When in reality, you just got a $65 client!

Now for the ones who want bare bones service: if you get a customer who still wants bare bones, watch them, watch them, watch them. Here's why: if it's a small business they might be doing sidewalks & de-icing themselves. You probably aren't going to change that. But for larger businesses that use the employees for this, you've got a chance.

For example: I have a rehab facility who said they'd take care of de-icing themselves. I came back by one morning after I'd plowed their lot and saw 2 of the office girls out there in their nice clothes throwing ice melt by hand. After a few snowfalls I stopped in & saw the boss. I told her I saw her girls out there throwing ice melt by hand. Followed with, you know that stuff isn't the greatest thing to get on your hands! I'm sure it doesn't do their clothes any good either. Then I said, you know, if you want I'll still take care of that for the price I quoted you. Then I throw out the 'spreader line.' Most of the time, I get them. What they don't think you know is, these girls have been chewing their ear off about doing this. But you've been 'watching them.'

Another one I do is this daycare who has a wheelchair ramp. It's about 50-60 feet long. The first year I provided service to them I charged $15 to shovel it. With solid 5ft walls on both sides of it, it was a real pain. The next year they said her girls would take care of that but if it got too deep they would have me do it. I explained that it would be a lot harder when the snow got too deep because of the walls on the sides & that since it was a 'as needed' removal it would be $25 instead of the $15 they had paid in the past. She said that was fine. But now I have a snow blower. The first time they called for the ramp I was in & out in about 10 minutes. $25 please! Thank you. Remember, if you're NOT doing it, SOMEBODY else is. Figure out who & use that to your advantage. Good luck!

Also, after my first year of plowing on my own & seeing exactly what my expenses where, I raised my prices the 2nd year & didn't lose a single customer. Good, friendly, service."

Tips for winning commercial snow plowing accounts.

Have you had difficulties landing commercial snow plowing accounts? It can be difficult to break through a companies many layers of insulation before you get to the person in charge of making such decisions. Persistence seems to be a big part of success. Let's look into this discussion that took place on the Gopher Lawn Care Business Forum.

A business owner wrote "landing a large commercial account is not the easiest thing to do but once you have them you can keep them for a very long time provided you are doing a professional job. The amount of money you can generate for your company from a single commercial client can be quite large over time.

I landed a few medium sized commercial snow plow accounts for this winter and have some good leads on summer work. I will be pushing for residential lawn care very heavily at the beginning of next year. My feeling is that my company WILL be successful in both residential and commercial accounts."

How do you feel you were able to land your initial snow plow accounts? Did you happen to know the decision makers or are did it come down to just being good at sales? Do you have any advice for others looking to land commercial snow plow accounts in their area? I am sure others would appreciate any insight you have.

"Landing the commercial accounts last year was just luck I guess. I am sure it had a lot to do with my approach and attitude for wanting to do the work. I did not know any of the decision makers when I first made contact. First, you need to spend a great deal of time finding out who is really in charge. Sometimes I will spend hours making phone calls just to try and get some contact information and that is just the start of the process to land a commercial account. I have one here in the area that I have been working on for two years now and have not landed any business so far. I will keep trying however because I want the account.

As far as advice for landing commercial snow plowing accounts I would recommend that you try and find someone who knows someone connected with the facility you are trying to land. Talk to your friends and family members because they all work somewhere and chances are, their company location will need the services you provide. These property managers get so many phone calls for services that if they don't know you, chances are you will not get to first base with them. I find that having a referral is the best way to make an initial contact. It gets your foot in the door and then the rest is up to you. Depending on the type of commercial account it is you might need to be available 24/7 during the winter months. There is a lot of prep work and a lot of behind the scene work that you need to do in order to perform a professional job.

This year has been very tough to break into commercial accounts. I had two large accounts that I have been working on for the past two years and I got the impression that I was in for this year. I got this feeling from conversations that I was having with the persons in charge. I spent three weeks trying to get a detailed quote together for one of them. They wanted the service quoted several different ways. It turned out that both told me they were staying with their current company.

My feeling is that with the economy as bad as it is this year, you have people trying to land accounts just to try to survive. Most are under bidding and I would guess that most will fall flat on their face when the time comes to service the accounts. You can not do a large account with a small pickup truck and a 7 foot plow.

One other piece of advice is that when I look at a possible account I try and decide how much I want to profit on the account before I put a bid together and stick by my guns. I will not take an account for little profit just to get the account."

How to get lawn care jobs from property managers.

One member of the Gopher Forum has got a great system set up to get work. He has been able to set up an infrastructure so that property management companies send him faxes of the work they want done, daily. It seems like a great way to run your operation and he was kind enough to share some of insight as to how to do this.

He wrote "right now I am working mainly with two property management companys. When I first started doing work for them, they used to have me give them a quote first before they approved it and I could begin the work. Now they just fax me the job and I will bill them monthly. Unless the jobs are more than $250, which I then need to give them an oral quote, and they usually just approve it and I get it done.

The work is mainly tree and landscaping work. A lot of tree trimming, irrigation repairs, and yard clean-ups. They also have me bid on weekly yard services for them that more often than not, I end up getting. I have found they really appreciate the jobs getting done quickly. If they have to wait a week or more, then they will call some of their other vendors.

Each day the faxes come in as a work order with the address, job description, and renters contact number. I check the fax machine when I get home at the end of the day, and fit the jobs in my schedule for the next day or 2.

The property management companies each manage about 1,500 properties, so you can imagine they have plenty of work to go around. It was fairly easy getting my foot in the door too and I don't know why more lawn care business owners don't do what I have done.

Here's what I did at first. I was driving by a home with an overgrown yard that had a for rent sign in the front lawn. I called the # and told them I could take care of the properties right now for them. They said I had to have my insurance and business license on file with them first (I already knew this). I struck up a little conversation with the lady so she would remember me. I took my paperwork in the next day and asked if they had any work right away. 'Not at the moment, but we'll call you', she said. I waited 2 days, called back and asked the lady again. 'Not at the moment,' she said again. I waited 2 more days and called again. 'Well, I do have this one…,' From that moment on I knew I was in. Since then, the work has been coming non stop. Persistence pays.

At least once per month I bring in either Starbuck's or fruit smoothies to all the ladies in the office. Around Christmas time I send them a basket, a Christmas card, etc. It doesn't cost me much compared to what they pay me, and it keeps me in their minds."

How to win over a property manager.

This is a very interesting topic. Lawn care business owners are always looking for ways to land commercial lawn care bids. But what's the best way to do it? There are many ways to go about getting close with property managers to win bids but there is nothing like hearing the inside scoop straight from a property manager himself. That is what we were lucky enough to hear in this discussion.

A lawn care business owner wrote "my question is how do I get commercial properties? Everyone tells me I have to go to them, they won't come to me. Before we get into this I would like to tell you about my business.

I started my lawn care business four or five years ago with about four accounts my first season and second season I got up to about ten. That's all I had for the next two seasons. So for this season I advertised with signs and that got me up to about twenty five accounts give or take. I moved up from a 21 inch push mower to a 36 inch commercial walk behind. I would like to expand into commercial businesses in my area because all I've been doing is residential yards. I'm wondering when to start looking for these commercial properties for next season and how to land them?"

Great question and here is some insight shared with us from a property manager. He responded "hello, I am a property manager of approximately 2 million sq ft of commercial space. I was reading this and thought I would throw in a few thoughts.

The company I work for prepares it's budgets between the end of August and beginning of September with final revisions in October. This is a little earlier than most, but not by much. Especially given today's economy, we are looking at every expense harder than ever before. One of the differences I did this year in accepting bid's/proposals was I wanted every item broken out.

In the past I would ask for the total year number, number of cuts and what that number included. I put together a bid package outlining what I want, and then get the number as a whole. This year I wanted every service provided broken out, a la cart. I am tailoring the service to my budget and cutting costs where I can. I am looking at everything from irrigation maintenance to fertilizer and tree trimming, trying to find small amounts that can be cut to make a difference. However small. Maybe this year I will only trim the tree's once and fertilize once instead of twice like last year. Not sure, but I need options right now.

I have met a lot of resistance from several contractor's telling me not to cut back on fertilizer or other services, but the fact of the matter is that the budget is so tight and the property incomes are so greatly reduced, every dime I can squeeze out has an impact.

Those landscape contractors that I invited to bid this year tended to get my attention about 6 months ago. Maybe by once a month sending me an email or brochure after a phone call. I actually throw out the ones that get overzealous, but that's just me. I don't need a call every week. Once a month is fine. I have a lot of other things going on, but again, that's just me.

Insurance is a priority. I am in large scale commercial property management and all of my contractors are required to carry 2 million in insurance. We used to take 1 million, but now only 2 million is looked at.

I require terms also. Sorry, but my office, on average gets 100 invoices a day. We handle approx 10 million sq ft, so lots of things need to be paid. It's just not possible for me to cut a check the same day or typically even a week to get someone paid. We require all contractors to be on a 30 day invoice. Obviously we are good sized and a lot of smaller companies can turn invoices around faster, but if you want our work, you have to meet the terms.

Lastly, and more than anything I look at is references. I require and call, references. Sorry, your brochure looks great, but I don't know you from Adam, so I need to talk to people that do know your work.

One last thing I would like to throw out there for thought is, this year has been bad for commercial real estate and the forecast for next year is going to be much much worse. I would caution you that there are a lot of real estate companies out there on the verge of closing and are having a hard time paying their bills, and for that reason may be making a fast switch because the place needs to be maintained, but they didn't have enough cash to pay the last guy. Just be wary of anyone making the 'fast switch' right now. I am also seeing a lot of companies stretch those 30 day payment terms into 45-60 days.

Again, we are pretty good sized and I'm sure that's not what everyone here had in mind about commercial, but I just thought I would try to contribute."

What fantastic insights. Now that you know all this, you can take this information and use it to your advantage when trying to get the attention of a property manager.

More secrets on winning over a property manager.

Here is the follow up conversation I had with a property manager on the Gopher Lawn Care Business forum. He shared with me some really important insights you must know as a lawn care business owner if you want to win him or others in the industry over and get them to accept your bid.

I asked "I do wonder as you reflect back on your dealings with lawn care companies. Do any specific things some of them did really help them stand out and win you over? Or did it all just come down to who could do the job for the lowest dollar value? Also, what kinds of things have lawn care business owners done that were an absolute waste of their time when they were trying to get your attention and market to you?

Could you also share with us the steps a lawn care business should take from how to initially contact the property management company to ultimately winning the bid? I am sure many readers would love to know how this works from your perspective."

He responded "first off, I don't think of myself as a price only customer. I am more than willing to spend the cash if the service is needed and worthwhile. That being said, we do look at the bottom line and try to figure out where we can save a few cents per sq ft. One of the reasons we like our bids broken down into specific services and their prices is perhaps there are some duplications in services I am receiving from different vendors.

For instance, our current landscape maintenance company picks up all the misc. trash around the property when they service the area. I love that, but I pay another company to do that three times a week, so is it possible for me to save a little if I ask you to cut that out? That's really where my effort has been in trying to cut costs.

As long as your price is reasonable, I am good with it. I know that sounds like I'm trying to cut corners but right now I am trying to compete with other landlords who are also trying to drop their costs to pass the savings along and get the few prospective new tenant's out there attracted to my property. Maybe this year I will plant annuals instead of every quarter replacing the entrance flowers etc. Those are the price issues I am addressing.

I've tried to think of some things that have/have not worked in getting my attention, but honestly, I have to say consistency, professionalism, you definitely need to show professionalism. No jeans and t-shirts please and make sure you follow up. Being consistent in your calls to me, or your follow up email is important. A lot of it, sorry to say, is right time and place, and if you are consistent about reaching out to me, you will be there at the right time.

I'll also throw out one of the best things I have had a landscape company do for me. After every service call to my property, I get a check list showing what was done, what needs to be done (along with costs) and when the next service call will be. That helps give me a picture of what's going on, so if I am asked any questions, I have the answers already and don't need to make a call to find out."

What great advice. To round out the conversation, another lawn care business owner jumped in and shared with us what has worked for him when trying to land commercial accounts.

He said "the best thing to do is get out and talk to managers/owners face to face. Spark up a conversation and ask if they are accepting any new bids for their lawn care and landscaping services. You will be amazed at how many business owners/managers are unhappy with their current lawn care company. Most businesses already have a lawn care company, so be prepared to not get a lot of commercial accounts the first year you go after them. If the business is not happy with their current lawn care company, they will usually be more than happy to let you know when their contract is up. Take some notes: What they expect, what they are unhappy about, and WHEN THE CURRENT CONTRACT ENDS.

Keep in contact with the people in charge (stop in and say hi, send a card around the major holidays) and submit a bid a couple weeks before the contract is about to end. Also have your act together: Company shirts, professional letterheads, business cards etc., clean cut appearance (present yourself as a business owner, not just a guy that cuts lawns), and have your insurance in order.

Remember a business wants to hire a professional company, not a guy in a truck with no insurance that doesn't pay taxes."

Create a check list to win over commercial lawn care jobs.

Here are a few great ideas on how to land commercial lawn care jobs by creating a check list.

One lawn care business owner asked "I need some help here. The new lawn care season will be coming and I was wondering how lawn care business owners find out which lawn care contracts are up for bids for commercial areas? I have looked at public notices in the newspaper and emailed property management companies with little to no luck. What do I need to do??"

A second lawn care business owner said "emailing is a good first step but don't stop there. You have to get your name in front of them and in their heads.

Pick up the phone to find out who you need to speak to. Get the name of the purchasing manager.

Pound the pavement to pay them visits. On your first visit, bring flyers, business cards, and photos of previous (current) lawn care projects.

On your second visit, bring your lawn care equipment. Invite the purchasing manager outside to see that you have the equipment necessary to complete their lawn work in a timely manner and with professional results.

Never take the first three 'NOs' as a defeat."

A third business owner added "I never take my trailer to a commercial lawn care estimate. I think you look smaller when you show up by yourself with a bunch of stuff. I did this once and was asked if I thought I could do it alone. I told them that due to rain I gave my guys the day off. I didn't get the lawn care job though. I like to go to the site an hour ahead of our meeting so I can walk the whole place. I make a list of what I see and make it a point to tell them that I would never allow this to happen.

To better do this, I came up with a list of 25 reasons for a property management company to switch to us. This is just a list of the most common problems I've seen in my time. This gives them something to judge their current contractor by. A lot of property managers don't even know their property has any problems until I point them out.

I just put in a bid for a local commercial facility's lawn and I was standing in the entrance for about 20 min. waiting for the head maintenance man to show. When he got there I had a list of 22 lawn care problems that I would fire my father for. Now he knows that we know what he needs without him saying a word."

Here are some of the items listed on my property survey checklist.

1) inconsistent trimming on viburnums

2) inconsistent trimming of boxwoods

3) vines growing up arbor

4) weeds growing through boxwood

5) lack of edging of jasmine

6) jasmine growing on entrance sign

7) low tree canopy

8) lack of tree rings

9) lack of round up or equivalent

10) dead or dying hollies

11) lack of bed edging

12) annuals need cut back

13) pond not mowed

14) myrtles need trimmed

15) ligustrums need balled

16) african iris over sprayed

17) irrigation boxes not edged

18) beds not edged

19) crack weeds

20) juniper die back

21) weeds in juniper

22) tree suckers"

Now not everything on this list may work in your geographic growing area but that doesn't mean you can't come up with your own list of 25 common lawn care problems. Use this list to point out what is wrong with the current property's lawn care condition. This should help show you know what you are talking about and help you land more commercial lawn care accounts."

How to get commercial snow plow accounts.

If you live in an area where you get a lot of snow and are looking to expand your lawn care business into snow removal, you may be thinking how to land commercial snow plow accounts. That was a question brought up on the Gopher Lawn Care Business Forum when a member asked "as part of our lawn care business, we want to get some snow removal customers… preferably commercial accounts. Any ideas who to target and how? We thought about churches or apartment buildings. Are there free lists out there? Any other thoughts?"

One of the things you could do is drive through your area and make a list of the different commercial location that you would like to service. We have a letter in the free letter section On the Gopher Forum that you can send to these properties to request to be put on their bid list.

But the best thing to do is to knock on the door and ask who is in charge of the property and who you should send such a letter too. You improve your chances of landing these jobs when you meet the people who make such decisions.

Another lawn care business owner suggested "when you are driving around town, take a photo of commercial signs that are posted in front of business, then when you get home take and put the information into a database. Also look in the yellow pages (book and Internet). Get on the internet and look for Realtors and find commercial listing for rent or sale, the broker should be listed with contact information. Add these to your database. Then in the slow times do a mass mailing. Not only for snow removal but for lawn care too. It may take you longer but it may provide you with a better return. It also sure beats spending big $$$ for a database put together by a big company, especially if your marketing budget is small.

A friend of mine utilizes this marketing technique and has had a big return doing this as a painter. My return is growing but at a slower rate. Just remember for every 100 letters you send out, you'd be lucky to get 10 calls for estimates and maybe land 1-2 jobs, but depending on the job and price it may be worthwhile for you to do this."

What do you suggest a lawn care business owner send to a potential customer to get them to sign up for snow plow services?

Should they send them a bid? Or what kind of wording would you suggest in a letter?

He replied "I took the invite to bid format letter template that you have on the Gopher Forum and modified it to my particular market. In the letter I requested to be added to their bid list for future snow removal and lawn care needs. Granted I only had a partial list of (75) and gave 2 estimates, but my goal was to confirm an accurate database of the mailing address. I only had one invalid address. Another mailing is going out the end of October, along with the previous 75. I will keep this up during the winter and then do a mass mailing in early Feb. I will keep sending them letters to keep my name in front of the broker. I look forwards to seeing this marketing strategy pay off in the spring time.

In reference to a bid or letter, for residential properties, I would send a letter requesting an invite to bid on the customer's account. Around here, you can not go to someone's property and knock on the door selling your services. It's call solicitation and is against the city code. But if a customer asks you to do a bid, that is fine. Also you want to get a good lay of the property you will be plowing and make a sketch of the place, take digital photos, maybe a aerial shot from one of the internet satellite mapping sites, so when it snows and every thing is hidden, you have a good idea where the obstacles are."

Do you suggest doing any follow up calls at all or going into the commercial establishments to find out who is the contact person for property maintenance?

"Definitely do follow up calls. When you call, ask for the person you sent the letter to. See if they received your letter and go visit the place you want to target if at all possible. Sometimes that is difficult because the person that's hiring may be out of the city or state. Brokers and Realtors have a short attention span. They will receive a lot of phone calls, letters, and walk in clients on a daily bases, so you need to keep your company name in the front of their mind."

Connections will make your lawn care business succeed.

Isn't it amazing how success in business and sales always comes back to the simplest of things. Networking with people. That's it. We sometimes seem to make this process so much more complicated than it needs to be.

Why do we do this? Why do we get away from the fact that it all comes down to meeting people, knowing people, networking with people? This is a topic we had discussed on the Gopher Lawn Care Business Forum.

One lawn care business owner wrote "connections and networking I believe are the key components to success in any industry. As we speak, I am trying to work my connections to land a fairly large commercial client in my area. You know how I landed the previous one? It all came down to connections and networking.

You have to be able to transfer your credibility to your potential lawn care customers. This is very important and it is essentially what happens when you get a referral from a customer. Credibility is something that you have to build up over time. It may take a while to build but once you get it, you need to protect it and not do anything to tarnish it."

Another said "it is how I have made every business I have either owned or taken over a success. Simply calling people in my network or people in power that I know to plant the seed about what my new business venture is always gave me such a jump start. From there it's all word of mouth. I can tell you first impressions on a cold call mean a lot if you are going after the guy that has the big bucks. The way you, your truck, and equipment looks means a lot to them. I base this view on the constant feedback I receive from customers. One home owner's association that hired me for their property care took a look at my truck and equipment set up and said, 'now that is the kind of equipment we want looking after our properties.' I know it costs and it can cost a lot but you have to raise the bar to get into the big buck areas.

Recently I did my last home and garden show of the season. It was an amazing success. While I was there I was selling my services to the local community members. To do this, I had all the various post cards on display for the different services I offer such as, Organic Lawn Care, Tree Cutting, Leaf Collection and a few others. I bet over 300 cards were taken and I noticed a lot of interest in the organics and excavation services, a few for wood chipping too!

As for sales, holy smokes, I have made more in the past two weeks doing that show than many people in this industry make in six months. I was shocked! I got 16 new snow plowing accounts for this winter because of it.

A few former clients of a previous business I had, stopped by my booth that I haven't seen in years. I talked to them and will pick up additional work now because of our discussion. To be honest, I had forgotten about them and they were right in this rich area where I do mowing and lawn care now. I did remember their name and they knew who I was right away. So it just goes to show how important it is to stay in touch with your network."

ADDITIONAL SERVICES TO OFFER

How a free snow plowing can help you sell more.

As we have seen in many discussions on the Gopher Lawn Care Business Forum, the better the network you have, the more you will sell. Getting started though can pose a very tricky problem. How do you develop up a network to sell to?

Well chances are, you already have a network in place, you just don't realize it at the moment. We all know people from our daily interactions. Through friends and family. Also through others who provide us services. Some people in our community will tend to have a larger network than others. For instance a local doctor is going to know a lot more people in the area than an office worker.

The doctor will also have more influence on those in their network because they are highly educated and speak from a position of authority. There are other community members who might have equal or greater influence however, those in the medical field tend to rank up there near the top.

How does knowing this help you? Well let's take a look at what one lawn care business owner did to harness his doctor's social network. This is something you can do too!

He wrote "this past week, I went to my doctor's office for my annual check up. He lives five minutes from my house. We generally have nothing more than a quick conversation but this time I asked him, 'who is keeping you plowed out this season?' He said he was doing it with an old snow blower. I said what if I gave you free service for the year? He said sure and then I went on to say we were looking for snow plow accounts in the area. In the back of my head I felt like I was going fishing to see what happens. This is a local community medical center, so guess what that doctor is now part of, my social network and yes he has already sent referrals to me. While I was there, I dropped off some of my snow removal post cards to him.

Pardon the pun but it's really having a snowball effect and I would like to think we all have a doctor, dentist etc we can talk to. These people are the main root connection in your community. Because like us, they build relationships."

There is so much great stuff here to talk about! So in this situation, you offer him free service for the year to kind of like pull him into your network and with him knowing it's free, he might feel more compelled to send you customers? Why do you feel he was chosen over others to give the free service to? Was there something about him or his position in the community that made him stand out most? Does it just come down to he has a lot of customers himself that are all local and he is a good beacon to promote your services?

"We offered free service to get his attention, then do an outstanding job and the rest falls into place. I would be willing to bet no other patient has done something like this and added if you know of anyone else looking for plowing or excavation service, we would really appreciate the referral. If it works out we will continue to do little free things for him, like lawn care or whatever.

Doctors, dentists, lawyers, accounting companies, tax return companies, they know the people in our area, tap into it and see what happens.

Next I plan on upselling him on our lawn care services for the spring. He already seemed interested in the organic products we use. I suspect he will sign up with us before long."

Window cleaning helps gain lawn care customers.

Lawn care business owners are always looking for additional services they can upsell to their current customer base as well as use as an enticement to attract new customers. Coming up with ideas though is not always as easy as you would think. Here is one creative idea that can help you on your way. A member of the Gopher Lawn Care Business Forum shared with us a service that he offers and has really helped him grow.

He wrote "before I got into lawn care, I was running a window cleaning business. I got into window cleaning and developed a decent route because residual income was crucial for me. After a while of doing that, I brought on a friend and his truck to begin offering lawn care. Once I got into that field, I thought to myself, how did I miss this industry for such a long time!? It's a great business to be in and is a great reoccurring service to offer.

Mixing window cleaning with lawn care has turned out to be a winner. I use a two-man crew; one guy (me) does the exterior glass while the other guy mows the yard. It is the perfect blend of services to throw the competition off balance and open the eyes of the potential client W-I-T-H-O-U-T having to under-cut the other guys.

I use window cleaning as an enticement, to get the customer to sign a residential property maintenance contract. Exterior windows are cleaned twice a year.

Offering this service bundle also helps attract commercial properties as well. Many stores and other commercial properties pay for weekly or bi-weekly window cleaning and ALL of them pay for lawn care. What I have learned is once a property has the windows cleaned professionally, they tend to wanna stick w/it.

In my sales pitch I point out how they will only have ONE invoice for both services and they love it. As my company grows, I would like to offer as many services the typical home owner will desire. Kind of like creating a spa for home care.

If you are interested in this, consider:
1) most small lawn care businesses do not have customers on contracts. Instead they get paid per cut. As a result, your revenue drops during the Nov/March season. Most of my current clients are rather budget minded, retired seniors. However, even THEY do have the disposable income set aside for lawns. Many of these people would love to have clean windows! Maybe they feel they can't afford both. I can use this to my marketing advantage and offer new customers FREE window cleaning done 2X (exterior) just for signing an annual property maintenance contract with me.

2) For the A-type clients, the ones who want good work done, I can raise the rates slightly, say $5 a cut and include exterior/interior windows.

3) Many lawn care customers can quickly drop a lawn guy for a 'better price' or their brother's son's girlfriend's father got into the biz. BUT can HE do windows?

There are a ton of ways you can use window cleaning to entice or 'bump' or up-sell.

Example: 7-11's have windows and lawns. It is not often they have a budget for window cleaning. BUT they do have one for property care. I have spent hours talking to managers who have issues with the yard guys blowing 'dust' all over the windows.

I went to one local convenience store and told the manager 'If you pull the soda bottles away from the inside windows, I'll wash the insides and outsides so YOU can see what a professionally cleaned windows looks like.' After I did that sales presentation, his area manager took note and wants to see the windows cleaned more often. Since then, I landed the property maintenance job and do the exterior windows weekly at NO charge. It takes me 10 minutes. I am determined to OWN all their store contracts in my area by years end.

In the future as I expand I want to offer all of these services:

1) Carpet/Floor cleaning
2) Window Cleaning
3) Yards
4) Power Washing
5) Blind Cleaning

One call will do it all."

Lawn care business owner offering janitorial services too.

The winter months can be difficult for the newer lawn care businesses to get through but one member of the Gopher Lawn Care Business Forum found an additional service he could offer that helps him pave the way to pick up more lawn care customers in the spring. He offers janitorial services.

He wrote "here is what I have been doing to drum up business. I went from a $100,000 liability insurance and switched it over to a million dollar liability policy.

Then I bought 2,500 postcards, bought some business mailing lists from around my area, went to the post office and bought 200 stamps. I slapped them on the postcards, tossed them into the mail box, and walked away. Today I received 7 calls to come in and talk, and I landed 5 bids! Now I'm in the janitorial side of life as well. I'm cleaning bathrooms and making making.

So let's recap shall we? The first time out was last spring when I first started my lawn care business. I bought all my equipment brand new. I have two of each, mowers, blowers, trimmers. I bought a trailer used, bought a brand new snow blower for $1,250. Bought 2 trucks, one is a 4×4 for the snow removal.

I was still working a full time job and working my lawn care business on the side. I worked like a tank but I had to make more money and I did. My secret?….Being friendly. Saying thank you every chance I got and telling everyone to have a good day, take care. That's all I did and I did good work. Handshakes to the Mr's and jokes to the Mrs.

Before I did this I had no clue about janitorial services, I just read a lot and followed some advice. Now I can keep myself as busy as I want to be and make the money I want with these additional services.

Most times it's easier just to do something then to analyze it to death.

What got this idea to offer janitorial services started was when I was think that all private offices and buildings have parking lots and grass. Where there is grass, there is money. Where there is a parking lot, there is money. So what if you have to clean a toilet??? Now let's take it further, why not offer parking lot cleaning and stripping.

I managed to get 15 new lawn care accounts with my janitorial services. Each janitorial bid I make can effect If I get the lawn and snow accounts too. I can then upsell other services like parking lot stripping. There are endless possibilities really. You have to ask yourself, how much do you want to work and how fast do you want to build your business? Because that's what it is all about. It's a business and I don't know about you or anyone else that is doing this as income but, I love money.

My kid will need money someday, and I really don't want my kid punching a time clock when she is 34 years old. If I bust my butt and build something good then she can take it if she wants to. I am not big time yet but, it might be good to start thinking I am because maybe it will push me into another direction to become big time."

These are all great ideas on ways to utilize your time when lawn mowing stops for the year.

How to get started offering holiday decoration and lighting services.

The winter months can be a tough time for a lawn care business. More and more lawn care businesses are getting into offering outdoor holiday lighting and decoration services to help them get through the slow times. Those who have experimented with it seem to be pretty happy with the results but how do you get started offering these services?

One lawn care business owner wrote "I'm just getting started in offering holiday decoration services and I'm really not sure how to go about bidding on hanging lights. I put a nice ad in my local newspaper and have been receiving responses. My going rate for lawn care is $60/hourly.

I am planning on my holiday lighting estimates to include both putting up and taking the lights down. I will be using the customer's lights as well. Should I possibly ask if I need to supply the product? I have a few customers already calling and I procrastinated how to deal with this."

Another business owner shared "since this is your first time doing this, why not decorate your own house with some lights and figure out how long it takes you to do some standard lighting, such as running lights across the roof line. Figure out how long it takes by the linear foot. This should then help you measure the time it will take you to decorate other homes, and businesses.

Then if you are going to be taking them down as well, you will need to double that fee. Why not try and keep your hourly rate for lawn care, the same in your lighting bids.

If you want to offer your own lights, why not consider figuring out how much lights are costing and buy them as needed. Charge the customer for the lights and then you will be able to take them down and reuse them next year as well. You could consider charging double the cost of the lights.

I charge by the hour. I sell the clients the lights or they buy them elsewhere. I put them up and take them down. When I take them down, I put them in some big plastic bin containers and put them in their garage. I know I could get a lot more because I've heard of guys doing a $1,000 a house or small business and being very basic. I've been charging like $300 for a better job. It's still new to me though. I have looked at some of the 'holiday lighting wholesellers' and they seem to be the same price as a box store, so I just purchase them locally. If the client owns the lights then you explain that every year they will more than likely have to buy a few new sets because they go out. Plus if they want to expand on it they can do so a few pieces at a time.

It usually takes me morning until lunch for a $150 job and $150 to take them down which takes less time. You can make a lot more but once again I am new to this and am figuring out my costs."

A third business owner said "my average job involved me installing 6 strings of 50 LEDS with a light clip for every light on a two story house/business. I charge by the hour and supply the lights. A simple light around the roof job will cost about $20 per box of lights and $5 dollars per box of 100 clips. It takes 5.5 to 6 hrs to install. I charge $380.00.

To become successful at this, keep experimenting with offering holiday lighting and decoration services. Try to increase your sale price with each customer as you go. As you get better with it, try and shoot for $750 to $1,000 per house/small business. This includes installing the decorations and taking them down. You can use your own decorations or use the customers. Try both ways and see which works best for you. To market this, I have used postcards and door hangers. It also pays to talk with people you know and see if they work at a location where holiday lighting would attract more customers and make them more sales."

Offering parking lot cleanups with your mowing bids?

If you are looking for more add-on services to market to your commercial clients, consider offering parking lot cleanups.

One lawn care business owner wrote about his experience with this service and said "I have been very busy lately and have some how gotten myself into a new aspect of commercial property care. A little while back I landed a parking lot plus mowing contract. As time went on, word spread about the quality of my work and I have been getting more calls from other commercial plazas in the area wanting my services. I utilize a hands on cleaning method for these parking lots and I am doing a much better job than the parking lot sweepers they have hired in the past. I do know for a fact that I will not be doing any residential lawn care accounts this year since I am so busy otherwise. I have set up a deal with another lawn care operator who lives near me, to do them. I will be working on Commercial Only!

You guys should try to offer parking lot cleaning services along with your lawn care accounts. If you do, remember to pick up all the paper trash, even if it's very small. That makes a big difference in the quality of your work and it will be noticed. I have 3 parking lots I am doing now for $1,600 a month per parking lot. My goal is to get a total of 15 by the end of the summer. It's not going to be too hard where I live. Multiply $1,600 a month x 15 and see what you get. Now you can understand what kinda money there is to be made.

The average lawn care business owner may wonder what kind of sweeper you need to have to clean parking lots. Instead of paying big bucks for a fancy sweeping system, I use one of those hand held pickup trash devices to get larger items. Then I use a walk behind blower to blow any other smaller trash away from the front of the store and I use back blower also. Afterward, I use my utility vehicle to drive around the parking lot sucking everything up with a portable vac system I mounted on the UTV. It makes for a very easy job."

A second lawn care business owner asked "can you explain exactly what your doing, are you basically walking around picking up any little piece of trash? Do you service these parking lots daily or how often? What sets you apart from parking lot sweepers that scrub and vacuum everything up?"

He responded "to me the difference is in the hands on cleaning. The larger companies do not get the trash from the parking islands. They do not get the leaves from the corner of the walk ways and so on. They don't pick up cigarette butts that litter the flower beds. It's the detail work that counts and that's what I do. I do them every other day.

To get yourself started, find out who owns your local shopping plazas and get in touch with the owner."

MARKETING TEMPLATE EXAMPLES

Lawn care business commercial property bid cover letter sample.

When your lawn care business is submitting a bid for property maintenance, consider including a bid cover letter along with it. It's a great way to look professional and improve your chances at winning the lawn care bid.

For example:

Mr. Smith
123 Main St
Anytown, USA 90210
(800) 123-4567

RE: Weekly Lawn Maintenance

Dear Mr. Smith,

Thank you for inviting John's Lawn Care the opportunity to submit this proposal to provide you with lawn care services for your property located in CITY, STATE.

The pricing bid for this property is outlined on the enclosed quotation sheet. The cost is based on weekly mowing, trimming, edging, and blowing down of all hard surfaces. Five (5) premium fertilizing applications and a spring core aerating. If you find any of this information to be in question please give me a call at xxx-xxxx.

Again, thank you for the opportunity to submit this proposal. We are excited to establish this new business relationship. We are looking forward to doing business with you this year and we are confident you will be extremely pleased with our services.

Sincerely,

John Thomas
Owner

End of lawn care season customer letter sample.

At the end of the lawn care season you may want to consider sending out a letter like this one. It is a great way to reach out to your lawn care customers and say thank you.

Homeowner
10 Any Street
Your City, STATE 87392

Dear Customer,

I would like to thank you again for choosing Smith Landscaping for your lawn needs. We hope you were more than satisfied with our performance. This season is at a close and this will be the last billing for the year. If you need any last minute services before winter sets in, feel free to contact us. We will be sending out a letter in March to welcome you back to the new season. Until then, we hope you and your family will have a safe and happy winter.

Sincerely,

Joe Smith
888-321-1234

Sample letter for Property Managers

Here is a sample letter posted on the Gopher Lawn Care Forum that your lawn care business could edit and send out to property managers to help you gain commercial lawn care accounts.

(888) ###-xxxx
1-29-XX

Thomas Beal
Beal's Lawn Care

Miss Clarke,

Hello, please allow me to take a moment of your time. My name is Thomas Beal and I represent Beal's Lawn Care.

I would like to be considered for any and all Property Maintenance contracts or jobs that you may have coming up this year. My company is professionally licensed and insured.

We have been in business and serving the area for over 10 years now. You can speak to me at any time, and be confident knowing that your needs will be addressed immediately. We offer mowing, edging, planting, natural & permanent mulch, retaining walls, and have recently included hydroseeding, erosion control, and spray-on-mat.

Please add me to your bidders list and please contact me for any size job you may be considering. I am always happy to give free estimates. You can reach me at (888) 555-1234 or email me at yourname@domain

Sincerely,

Thomas Beal

LESSONS LEARNED

What I have learned in my lawn care business.

There is nothing like learning from those on the front lines of the lawn care industry. They are the ones in the trenches, putting ideas, equipment, and know how together to keep their businesses going and growing. Here are some great insights from a member of the Gopher Lawn Care Business Forum who is out there battling everyday to make his business not only survive but thrive. Maybe some of his tips will help you with a situation you currently find yourself in.

He wrote "I have grown my lawn care business from nothing. When I got it started, I hated my job and I wanted more out of my life. I needed a mower for my house anyway so I decided why not start a lawn care business and see what I can do with it? From this experience, I have tried a lot of things and made many mistakes that I have learned from. Here is a list of what I have learned from operating my lawn care business.

The first mower I purchased was a big box consumer grade zero turn mower. The mower was not designed for heavy usage and it led to break downs every week. Using consumer grade equipment for professional use is something that should be AVOIDED at all costs. As soon as I could, I traded up for a commercial zero turn, and never had a problem again.

I try and base my lawn care business on things I learn from all other businesses. I learn from everywhere I can. I will pick any business and think of the things I like or don't like about it. For instance, take Mcdonald's. You get affordable prices, and you're in and out quickly. EVERYONE eats at Mcdonald's so they are doing something right. On the other end of the spectrum, look at a Perkins, they take longer, and the price is higher, but you get more of a selection, better quality, and better service. I look at every business and look at what makes them work and try and incorporate as many of their good things into my business as I can.

That being said, there are people out there that try and do a business without proper equipment. From my experience, you shouldn't be running a commercial business with consumer grade equipment. Either make a go of it and go all in or don't go into it at all. You would be surprised how fast word gets around in your area. If a new business opens up and offers bad service, and quality, you will quickly find people talk about it and let others know the service was wasn't good. But if you use commercial equipment, have a good appearance and offer good service, the word passed on will be that you have to hire this reliable lawn care company. So keep in mind that EVERY first encounter is important.

At first, I worked a full time job, and mowed on the side. After I saw the potential of my lawn care business, I started mowing full time. Picking up yards as I went. ANY new business needs to understand that by under pricing yards to get work you are hurting yourself and the whole market around you. Your cost may not be very high, and you can mow cheaply at first, but soon enough, you will find your expenses go up as you go legit and have to pay for things like taxes and insurance. Or you will find your truck is having problems, your house will flood, your insurance will go up, you will have a child. So don't overlook the fact that this business needs to pay for all of your business expenses and it must pay you.

If you figure $10 bucks an hour for yourself, that's not a livable wage. You might have gotten paid that at your full time job but you didn't have to pay any costs to run the business you worked for. Now you do. Another thing to keep in mind is that as a business owner you don't work 40 hr weeks anymore. You will work closer to 100 hour weeks.

I have learned that building your lawn care business too fast is a bad idea as well. At first, I jumped in and got an f-150, it turned out to be not enough truck. I went into the dealership and traded it for 2 cube vans that I could drive my mowers into. It's a great set up, but now my payments went up along with my insurance. Shortly after that, I found myself needing a dump truck for leaves and landscaping. When you look at the 2 huge trucks and a dump truck and the zero turns and all of the things, my month to month costs skyrocketed and made it near impossible to get by.

Employees are a scary thing as well. With employees, you are taking someone else's life into your hands. If something breaks down and an employee needs to get paid, you need to be able to work without that equipment. You must care for your employees the way you care for your equipment. You need to put money into it to keep it working, gas, and oil. Every once in a while you add an attachment, a striper, a bagger, you need to take care of that employee the same way. Buy them lunch, or a soda at the gas station, treat them well. If you lose a good employee you have to start from scratch again, find another employee and re-train them. The more you do this, the more time and money will be spent on the process.

Use tools that help you save time. Gopher Lawn Care Software has been a LIFE SAVER for us. Without this program I would be lost. I work all day, everyday. I put things off and no software can make up for human laziness. I have a house full of papers, a garage full of mowers, a town full of customers a brain full of ideas and somehow I gotta squeeze a life into that.

I am heavy on the residential side right now. In the future I want to be all commercial, but I have noticed that a lot of those are bid every year. There is no customer loyalty with commercial lawn care customers. If someone comes in and under bids me I am out of work.

I have done a lot work and won a lot of commercial bids. One lesson about dealing with commercial customers that stands out to me is, if you call in or stop in and have a question about how they want a certain property issue handled and the answer isn't from a supervisor, don't take it. I have called places and they have left a note about an issue, I never heard back from and then I hear they took a bid from someone else for the job, who is 45 min away and is charging way more than I would have.

How do you find the correct person to talk to with commercial work? When is the right time to bid on commercial jobs? I have found that most apartments are owned in groups. You need to go in and find the specific person in charge of taking bids. Once you do, you may find they also are in charge of other properties in the area.

I struggled with landing town homes and home owner association lawn care bids. With these organizations, there are boards and many people in charge. There were just way too many folks to deal with to make it worthwhile for me. Too many people to complain about too many things. I would rather have one person to deal with.

I like using the lawn care price calculators on the Gopher Forum as well since they are helpful. Knowing what you need to make is key, especially if you are sitting in an office while others mow. You MUST make money on every job. I have talked to a few other business owners that say you should take the good with the bad, but I disagree. Even if you are breaking even, that is not a profit and you need to get out. We do this to make money.

Advertising is tough where I am. I pass out 100 flyers and get 1 call. I put an ad in the paper and get a lot of calls, but the paper just keeps raising their prices. Next up is advertising only on the internet to gain work and through word of mouth.

If you need to raise a price, have a list of things you can use to help explain why. Don't make excuses, like I said we do this to make money. Be able to explain to the customer that the tires on your truck are $200 bucks a piece and you need 4 of them. Or maybe that insurance went up, gas went up, whatever it is. Don't raise a price and have no reason to explain why if they ask.

I know I do A LOT WRONG, I try to fix things as I go and study whatever I can to get better. I realize no business will be perfect but I try to constantly broaden my knowledge base."

My HUD housing mowing nightmare.

Here is a classic tale of what can happen when you are too eager for work. Some lawns are unmowed because the cost to mow them is just too high. You always have to visit each and every property you are bidding on, before you submit your bid. If you don't and you are too eager to bid sight unseen, there is a very good chance you will pay for your mistake. As we will see in this story from the Gopher Lawn Care Business Forum, it's better to work smart than to work hard.

A new lawn care business owner wrote "I started my lawn care business late in the season so when I got a call replying to an internet classified ad from a property management company that managed 30 HUD properties, I jumped at the opportunity. They were offering me the opportunity to bid on all 30 lawns at $35 a piece every two weeks. After some quick negotiating, I got 10 of the lawns up to $60 per cut due to the distance from my home.

I was so very excited about all this new found work until I saw what I was dealing with. I started the first week of June and almost immediately became aware that none of the lawns had been mowed at all this entire year, and some for two years! They were all jungles. Some of the grass was as tall as me (5′9″). These jobs were better suited for a bush-hog that I didn't have. But I refused to quit and I grabbed my cheap 25cc curved shaft weed eater and after about three weeks the first brutal round of cuts was complete.

With all that hard work put into those lawns, I tried to renegotiate the pay for the initial cut but was unsuccessful. One day after I had completed the first round, I got an email informing me that the price was dropping to $25 per lawn. I pleaded with the crooks but they knew they had me and wouldn't budge. But I still refused to quit.

It's been about two months now and the jobs are much easier. I've upgraded my weed eater and am about to get some more equipment. I'm now hiring people to do the larger lawns while still bringing in a small amount of profit from them while I personally handle the smaller, less time-consuming lawns. I now have 33 HUD lawns and I'm enjoying the work. But it's still not all roses.

The company I have the contract with now owes me about $3,300. They use a net 30 payment process, which sucks. You get paid 30 days after you complete all the lawns, submit before/during/and after photos, and submit a spreadsheet with dates. What's crazy is that I am still waiting for my first pay check. After inquiring, I was told it was mailed 8 days ago. This is a very big problem for me as I have no credit cards and no money left, so I had to put all the jobs on hold until I get paid.

This whole thing has been very stressful and has required intense physical labor that only a crazy person would attempt for such low pay. I've heard many other stories where the people were paid fairly and the jobs weren't so terrible, I just don't have one to share with you. Overall, I'm glad I agreed to the deal, I've learned a lot and most of my bitterness will fade away once I start getting paid, if I do. I'd definitely take another deal like this if the pay was a little bit higher.

If I had it to do over again I would have done some things different. First off, I would have traded in my minivan and all other valuables for a sturdy ztr mower. With the desperate situation I was in, there wasn't much else I could do if I wanted to succeed. Starting out late in the season with very little investment money and no credit but bad credit left me in a tough spot. So when the crooks called, I jumped at the offer.

Right now, I'm eating nothing but ramen noodles and waffles. My rent is 3 weeks late, I frightened the postal worker yesterday when I lunged at her from behind the dumpster trying to find my paycheck, and the crooks are pushing me to finish by Wednesday.

Also, I owe my helpers a good chunk of change and they're probably calling me awful names behind my back.
If these management company crooks weren't so far away from me, I could send somebody over to make them an offer they couldn't refuse but unfortunately all I can do is beg from my phone.

Be careful who you take jobs from. A lot of smaller clients may ultimately be a better way to go than one big client. At least with a lot of smaller clients, you can pretty much guarantee you will get paid on time by the majority of them."

Marketing lessons we can learn from a realtor turned lawn care business owner.

If there is one group of local business people who I find are constantly hammering me with direct mail marketing material, it's realtors. They really seem to have their act together when it comes to promoting their name and face out to the local community. So lucky us when a new Gopher Lawn Care Business Forum member joined up to say hi to everyone and shared with us his story on how he got started with his lawn care business and some marketing secrets he learned as a realtor.

He wrote "I just wanted to say hi and introduce myself. I'm just starting my lawn care service and to be honest I am a little nervous. I got here on accident, after being a real estate agent for years before my business was killed by the housing crunch, so I decided to start up a business I knew I would really love. To promote myself, I did what I knew best, network marketing. By reaching out to people I knew and others I met I was offered work cleaning up bank owned homes. Well after you clean them up you also have to provide lawn service. The banks want two cuts a month for $100.00. Right now I have 17 homes, so I decided to expand it to regular homes. I have a lot to learn but we are excited and ready to roll."

What kinds of things do you feel you are able to bring to your lawn care business from your previous real estate and network marketing business? I am sure you learned a lot of great marketing concepts.

"Thanks! I learned a lot about marketing in real estate, but the most important thing is you can't beat a referrals from a happy customer!!! Way back in the day when my wife and I started out in real estate, we had no budget, so we made up a flyer's that we dropped off on door steps. We picked a good geographic area with 200 homes. We made our flyer include cool and interesting facts. We also included a recipe of the month and what the housing market was doing. People loved it, but you have to know that you must hit a person 6 to 9 times to be noticed and you have to stand out.

Another tool I utilized was the fridge magnet, which are a great marketing tool. One of the best fridge magnets I have used is a fridge calender for clients, so your name is always on their mind. Constant contact is key, and follow up with this line:

OH BY THE WAY…
I'm never too busy for your referrals!!

Following these simple marketing steps allowed me to reach out and perform lawn care services for both residential and commercial customers."

The danger of large lawn care accounts.

It seems like every year I hear a similar story in different variations. A new business is just getting itself stabilized with a handful of customers when a large account seems to be calling them from up high atop a mountain of promised money. The call becomes so enticing that the entrepreneur can not stop themselves from holding back.

Does the beginning of this story sound familiar?

This time the story revolves around a lawn care and fence installation business. The business owner wrote "I had been in business over a year with just me running it with a helper from time to time. I also had a full time job to cover his expenses. All was going fine. The business was growing slowly until that fateful phone call came in. This large commercial property needed lawn care and a fence installed.

The job was going to be a big job but I was going to have to float the project for 60-90 days. That is how long it would take to get my first payment. The caller asked if I could do it? A big fat five figure project was just waiting for me if I said yes. So I gambled and said what the heck, I deserve this, this is my time to step up, and I said yes.

At the time I started this job, I had managed to save a few thousand dollars. I thought this would be enough to get myself and a few helpers through the next 2 month or so. The next day, I quit my full time job and showed up to this commercial facility to start work.

The grass was tall and unkept so it took more time than normal to cut it down. The fencing. Where do I begin. The fencing was going to cost big money that I didn't have. I knew I would have to pay for this on my credit card. I would also have to buy a large commercial mower on a credit card as well. But there was no risk right? I mean I would most certainly make my money back on all this and then some, right?

Within a day from the time I took the call, I had quit my steady full time job. Hired a few extra helpers. Depleted my savings and gone into a 5 figure credit card debt.

After the first month I submitted my invoice and was elated. Never had I submitted such a big invoice to anyone in the past. I was finally a big lawn care business. I already had plans to upgrade my truck and trailer. I felt like I had made it.

The second month rolled on and I started to get nervous, especially when I saw the for sale sign go up at the commercial location. I called and asked about that. Surely I was still going to get paid right? Oh sure they said, you will be paid. I was getting worried because I figured I had about 3 more weeks of living on my various lines of credit before I was maxed out.

Now do you want to guess what happened next?

The check never came. The commercial property was sold and I never saw 1 penny. I lost it all. I had to quit working on my business and get another full time job. And I will never ever be able to start another business again. My wife has threatened me with divorce if I ever brings it up.

Listen to me when I say this. There is a non-stop supply of such stories going around. Prevent this from happening to you. Start small and scale up. Grow at your own comfortable pace. And what ever you do, don't put all your eggs in one basket."

How would your lawn care business compare to this one?

Every lawn care business is different, just like every business owner is different. Some are out there doing the bare bones minimum and getting paid only a bare bones minimum price. But there are others who take their lawn care business to a new level. A very competitive and professional level. I am very happy to have gotten a chance to talk with this lawn care business owner on the Gopher Lawn Care Business Forum, about his operation because I think it will help you improve your game.

He wrote "I used to use a walk behind style mower which could only bag and not mulch. Now with my new 60″ ZTR mower I pull up next to other companies with just 1 employee. These competing companies often have 3 employees and usually are already on site when we come to service a neighboring property.

More often than not, we are able to mow and leave before they are done and our lawns look better hands down. There are only 2 companies in town who use stripers on the back of their mowers. My lawn care company is one of them. This is one of the ways my business stands out. I hope to gain a much higher customer base each season because I know the last year we were seen all over town making lawns look amazing with the 60″ mower. I am confident that this season will be the best one yet!

Having a striper that is designed to only fit your mower is important. In my opinion they are the best way to go. Mine has a lever next to my brake which allows me to lower and raise the striper and it is spring loaded. My mower stripes darker than anything I've ever seen. I have it on the lowest setting. It's a solid metal bar and comes with brackets to attach to your anti-scalp wheels. The bar becomes one big anti-scalp mechanism too. No more scalping over tops of hills with this.

When I mow a lawn all season, I start out by mowing it the same direction the first 2 times. This is all after de-thatching is done. I mow in only 2 directions for about 8-10 visits, and then I go a new way leaving those to pop through for a few weeks. I will alternate back and forth on a 10 visit ratio with only 2 angles to choose from at a time."

Ok so on your first visit you de-thatch? Then you mow the same direction for two visits. When you say you mow only 2 directions for about 8-10 visits do you mean to create the stripes? How does that differ from the first two visits you make when you go the same direction?

Then you go a new way? Like maybe the opposite diagonal?

"Picture this: I mow straight with the house for 2 visits to leave some dark bold stripes. After that, I mow horizontal with the house. I alternate between these 2 ways for about 8-10 visits. Then about halfway through the summer, I stop going those ways and I begin going diagonal. Because my mower is so heavy, being a full size ZTR, it would leave tire ruts if I went 2 ways all season. Alternating between 4 angles at once usually doesn't allow them to pop out as much.

All my lawns still have stripes in the winter just because I always go over the exact same stripes with no overlap. I see many companies who overlap over old lines and they end up making a mess."

I think you have fantastic results! How do you feel you are able to leverage these results with your marketing to promote your services? How do you feel you use this to stand out?

"I have a welcome kit that I give to all new customers. In the kit it has different sections. In the maintenance section, I make a point about the turf striper and the 'ball park' appearance I create on any lawn. A lot of customer's say they like the 'lines' the mower makes. It pretty much speaks for itself. At nighttime, all the houses I mow are eye popping. Like black and white stripes under the moonlight. Stripers will definitely make your work stand out."

What sections do you suggest a new lawn care business owner include in their welcome kit?

"Welcome kits should include different sections for all the services you offer. Combine pictures with facts and offers in small paragraphs. I also include an 8 page welcome letter. I give a broad description of services and they know they can call me for a free estimate anytime, and I will always be happy to meet with people, as well as return their calls within an hour usually.

I don't really think I need to put all the services I offer in great detail, brief descriptions along with pictures seem to do a better job. I also have pages for hardscape, excavation, softscape, and snow removal.

The welcome kit front page is a brief paragraph thanking them for choosing my company, followed by a paragraph about myself and the history and outlook of the company. The front page should include a mission statement with a short bio about you and your company. Your logo as well."

In Conclusion

Now that you are armed with all this wealth of knowledge, get pumped, get out there and make it happen. You have heard a lot of great insider secrets that most competitors would never share with you, so use it to your advantage.

Until the next time we meet, always remember to dream it, build it, Gopher it!

Sincerely,
Steve

CPSIA information can be obtained at www.ICGtesting.com
Printed in the USA
LVOW07s1245250115

424275LV00001B/341/P